simple
WONDERS
& a memorable year

by JCdeMelo

Contents

~ ~ ~ *Memories are sometimes recorded as a tribute to courage*

or kindness or generosity of spirit, sometimes they are told to

set the record straight or to create a sense of community.

Many stories collected through personal history are of an ordinary

person's experience of an extraordinary event in life – personal or

historical- and are often collected once the realization is made that

the storyteller won't always be around. ~ ~ ~

April Bell, Tree of Life Legacies

The Year That Was – My Memoirs

I am old, so I do not buy green bananas.

A. Souza, a friend of mine

Year 2011, part planned, part "it-just-happened", turned out to be quite a year to remember. And to revisit, if some of our future undertakings come close to this year. I doubt it, for we are running out of time, and money costs money. (Well, so to speak.) I guess it was a year worth writing about, at least this book as an outcome could provide for some reading food for our grand kids, once Donalda and I are gone. The year presented us with many of life's little and ordinary stories, vignettes which when bound together, strung like the beads of a rosary, form the whole thing.

The sad part is that it is hard for me to sit down and write. Sitting down alone is not attractive to me. This is my dilemma - that the mere mention of a distraction, and then more distractions, added to a lack of will and discipline, have often won the battle over the writing thing. I guess real, serious writers do not have these handicaps. Too bad for me, because I like to write.

And so it was that I forced myself to put the year in writing. Even if I had no plan, I had a bunch of loose notes and some pictures taken at random. These would be enough raw materials to get this writing project out of the train station and moving along the tracks. Eventually, I thought, it would take some shape and actually arrive at a destination. Pictures would not be enough; only writing would come close to doing justice to this bunch of stories of a wholesome and very full year.

2011 did have its preplanning. There were places to be and see, dates to follow, people to meet and participate with and informal budgets to obey. All of the elements of trip-taking were at play. Yet when the outcomes were very rewarding and unforgettable, the credit belongs to the unknown, the unplanned, the spontaneous, or just what we allowed to impact us with no questions asked or second thoughts contemplated. As it is often said: Just let it ride, baby. Let it ride.

1

Death in the Family

Happiness is beneficial for the body
But it is grief that develops the process of the mind
Remembrance of Things Past
Marcel Proust

Most people that live beyond ninety years of age are likely to have done a few things right, have navigated almost risk free and have some sort of endurance genes. However, in my opinion and from what I have read, this age also comes with many end-of-the-line attributes: you are ready to say goodbye, you are plugging along with good health supervision, and you are determined to challenge the sustainability of social security's benefits. (Well, I made up that last one.)

My mother-in-law passed away at age ninety-four in February 2011. Eight years earlier, we thought her living journey would go beyond a hundred. She, a widow for about twenty five years then, had been living with us for about eleven years, but then in 2002 some blood vessels problem called for surgical intervention, and from that point on she never regained normal health. Somewhat paralyzed and with some dementia, this became a downhill condition which demanded 24/7 health care. The initial months proved to be very challenging for my wife and her sister and an assisted living facility, albeit a very good one, run by Catholic nuns. Actually the idea was for New Bethany, the rest home, to become her own home. Although the rest home was located more than an hour away from all of us, she continued to receive loving attention from all members of the family, but in particular her two daughters. Her death was not received well. A better way to measure the loss is best described in the eulogy by one of her grandsons, on behalf of her two daughters.

Farewell To Rosalina, An Outstanding, Loving Mother And Teacher
-From Your Daughters

"I'm here today to share a farewell tribute to Rosalina from her daughters – Donalda & Donatilde. I'm standing in for them, because understandably the emotions of their mother's passing are great and delivering this message would be difficult. These are their stories, thoughts, and words.

Just last Saturday after visiting Rosalina at the hospital, Tony, one of Rosalina's many grandchildren, told Donalda – "Mom, I am at peace with myself. I am glad I stopped procrastinating in bringing little Nicholas to see Avó, to present to her... the youngest of her SIXTEEN great grandchildren."

Tony went on to say, "*Avó* is not the same woman that I used to know. It is sad to see her saying good-bye. I will miss her dearly."

It was sad to be witnessing the beginning of the end slowly unfolding before us. Yet, she was not ready then, last Saturday. She still laughed at things we said and smiled at faces that smiled at her. She would last a few more days, her heart, strong as a rock, resisting the fading away. Her heart was in command, till the end.

Even away from the comfort of our home and the daily interaction with any of us - she was not physically, emotionally, and geographically, very far from us.

During the last eight years, Donalda & Donatilde made almost weekly visits to New Bethany, in Los Banos, to see Rosalina. These trips, sprinkled in with other visits from family members and friends during this time, allowed her and us to find suitable comfort.

Originally resisting the change, Rosalina came to rely on everyone at New Bethany to bridge our visits. The Portuguese speaking sisters, and the peaceful sanctuary of the New Bethany chapel, which was the venue for her prayers and conversations with God, made missing her family more acceptable. Our family is grateful to the Sisters & staff of New Bethany for their spiritual gifts and professional, loving, and warm care for Rosalina.

Going further back in time - Shortly after we moved from San Lorenzo to this area – San Ramon - in 1976, Rosalina and Deniz went back to live temporarily in the Azores. Upon their return about five years later, we found a home for them, also in San Ramon. Besides wanting to be close to us, they expressed a strong desire to live near a Catholic Church. St. Joan of Arc, a new church and parish, was right across the street from their home - and became a blessing of untold rewards. Even with her limited English, Rosalina became a fixture - a wonder of sorts - at the parish. Her body language, and her neat and warm manners, became a notable endearment to her fellow church-goers. We were proud of her for capturing this attention that we could only admire.

Definitely - the last eight years have obscured the value that Rosalina represented and meant to all of us. She became a receiver of our attention, help and care - as opposed to the previous years when we saw her always the giver.

While it is normal to see or remember her for what she was lately, it is not difficult, on the other hand, to rewind the clock and revisit what she represented to all of us during the ninety plus years of her life. Not difficult at all. Figuratively, literally or explicitly - she was a giver. Ever giving of her love, counseling, and help.

As a highly skilled seamstress, we gambled that she would last forever and would always be around to supply us – the whole family – with her sewing, altering, and clothes fixing skills.

We remember the time she spent in all of our homes, fixing even the most insignificant pieces of clothing. Socks or underwear, logically against our will, received her professional attention and turned out like new. Yes....even holes in socks, or tears of seams, or imperfections of any kind would get a fresh and nice look. She was really good.

They lived a modest life, and were raised in a farming community in São Miguel. 80% of the island was poor and the rest of the population was less poor. They were self sufficient and somewhat sure of their destiny. Their mother, as a seamstress, assisted their father in managing the household by the economic standards of the time. In their periodic visits to the old country, it would be normal to hear ladies; young girls like them back then, praise their mother for teaching all of them to be equally competent seamstresses.

This praise was music to their ears, and they can fondly remember the time when they were the best dressed girls in their little village – *Lomba do Pomar*. With little money but with a great creative mind –

Rosalina dressed them very nicely. Their mother, a *Teixeira*, a proud and self-assured woman, contrary to their father, a *Pimentel*, a humble and easy going man, would rejoice in seeing them dressed well, the finished product of her skills.

With all this about their mother, there were aspects about her that remain forever deposited in our minds, hearts, and souls. They are the blue print of her character and the legacy of her teaching. These traits and inheritance of values are the ones that we cherish the most. They should - for we try to pass them along to our children and grand-children.

Her manners, her personality, her way of being were wrapped around a respect for all - do-as-you-must and stay within the boundaries kind of decency. She was a woman that prided on being *recatada*, which means one who behaves like a lady. She was prudish but allowed other more progressive behavior around her. Occasionally, John or Guilherme would venture into this unchartered territory - but she would accept it, as she loved and valued both of them tremendously.

Apart from their height – or lack thereof, she would remind her daughters with unequivocal honesty that they were very lucky to have them be a part of our lives.

Being such a close family, their mother knew everything about them – Donatilde's and Guilherme's, Dennis and Delia's, and John and Donalda's lives. It was a famous encouragement or plea from Rosalina when we were involved in some sort of argument, for her to say: "Try to live like *'Deus com os anjos.'* " Like "*Deus e os anjos*," which means you must try to live like "God and the Angels."

94 years – that's a long time. Rosalina lived a good life and was able to witness first hand, significant changes in her two worlds, her "homes" in São Miguel and in California.

She has known the joy of marriage, raising a family, and being bestowed with the blessings of numerous grand-children and great grand-children. She has suffered the pain of losing the most important person in her life, her husband Deniz. And living without him for almost 23 years – Ah, Deniz.

More recently, in 2008, she lost a son (Dennis), and a grand-daughter (Anna). We never told her. But we all knew that she knew – because she knew everything.

She was a big fan of the family gathering – sharing a meal that would somehow bring us closer together. Her *galinha com arroz* would do just that. At these events, one of the grand-children would invariably call out *vamos comer*, and a HUGE smile would appear on her face.

She was a very proud woman – proud of her family - without being boastful. She was always respectful of others.

As we have said many times – she was small in stature but she towered over all of us.

She was strong - and she was quiet – but she spoke up when she needed to.

She did not know how to drive, but at times she drove us crazy!

She did not know how to swim, but she would risk her life in a heartbeat to save someone else.

She did not particularly care to have pets in the house, but was perfectly comfortable having a pig – in the backyard.

She let us have our way, but deep down we knew she was the boss.

We all loved her very much. She may not be here in body, but her spirit will live on forever.

It is important for us to always tell her story, share her life, and celebrate her to our grand-children, great-grandchildren, relatives, and friends.

While we we'll all miss Avó tremendously and her passing is a great loss to us, we have been blessed to have had her for so long. She lived 94 good years, each and every day devoted to God. While she has passed from us, she has now passed to God. She lived for her family and God.

We should rejoice in her long life and that she is now with God to whom she prayed every day without fail. And we should rejoice that she is now reunited with her beloved husband, Deniz, her cherished son, Dennis and her precious grand-daughter, Anna.

Our whole family thanks all of you that knew her for joining us in this sad yet, equally happy "farewell" to a woman that we respected, admired, and cherished.

May her soul rest in peace – God's peace. Amen."

Rosalina at New Bethany

Rosalina in early 2000; taken at grandson Victor's wedding

2

Three Months Away

You don't write because you want to say something;
You write because you have something to say

F. Scott Fitzgerald

Three months in the Azores, Continental Portugal and northern Spain were on my calendar and my radar as late, or as early, as winter 2010. The pilgrimage to Santiago of Compostela - walking a portion of the French itinerary (*Camino Francês*) - had been in the works since 2008, shortly after my friend Viegas and I had completed the Portuguese route (*Camino Português*). The years 2009 and 2010 were filled with many family members and friends paying a visit to us at our home in San Miguel. Those visits by themselves, spread throughout two months, each of those two years, were all the time we could take. Our commitments in the US were greater than the desire to walk the *Camino*. The *Camino* fever had to be contained, in remission, for some time.

The pilgrimage was billed as the front and center of my 2011. Whatever else was on the menu would have to take care of itself if it came knocking at the door. Adding value to the Santiago thing was learning about and participating in an event that came to influence Donalda's desire and commitment to also do the *Camino* pilgrimage.

The 14th annual *Gathering of the American Pilgrims on the Camino* was going to take place in late March, just a few days before our departure to Boston to attend a Luso-American Life's event. A wise person would say no to too much of a good thing, to too much traveling. Besides, the time and money were an issue. Small, but an issue, never-the-less. *The Gathering* was a surprise, as my knowledge about the *American Pilgrims on the Camino* was zilch, nada, niento. I happened to learn about them by accident when searching for places where one could obtain a Camino Credential here in America, as opposed to getting it at the starting point of the Pilgrimage.

"Let's do it *all*." That was the unequivocal consensus of two (my wife and me), that was the command, or let's say, the verdict. At our age, even if there was no precedent in our past decisions and choices, being conservative at this time was not a good idea, we surmised. Things spectacular, against the grain or exotic never appeared on our resume of vacations and travels. Conservative, well thought-out and economy minded plans were more our style. So then, what's one more weekend and get away expense? After all, the setting was at Mission Santa Barbara. Donalda loved that idea, and that venue – a mission, and Mission Santa Barbara.

The *Gathering of the American Pilgrims* in Santa Barbara was exactly what the doctor ordered, both to validate my own Pilgrimage plan and to give birth to Donalda's commitment for a future Pilgrimage. If it were not for my commitment to include Viegas as my partner on the walk of 2011, Donalda would have joined me instead. Granted that the walk would be shorter, or with a changed itinerary, but Donalda would have been in.

The *Gathering*, in spite of its "it-looks-and-tastes-professional" approach, had nothing but simplicity written all over it. Good human touches abounded that long weekend. The stage was set with the Thursday evening registration and hospitality session; it signaled to us that this would be not just good, but refreshing. We needed such an introduction. Of course, *Camino* Walkers enjoyed one (perhaps two) glasses of wine and delicious hors d'euvres. Great start. Learning about the many aspects of the *Camino* phenomena added a lot of value to our already known love for the *Camino*. The historical, the spiritual, the tales and legends, the cultural ideas - all were shared well, some by people who had done research, and others who had experienced pilgrimage after pilgrimage. The *Gathering* was both good, and fulfilling. A quiet electricity sparked quickly between us. We were now ready for the *Camino* walk.

Our five days in Boston, with the Luso event as the trigger to begin our three months away from home, signaled that we were retired and making a soft transition to a freer life, a life we had dreamed of and thought would be possible. We visited more of New England and saw more relatives, particularly some we had not seen for a while. We were living our age. Not large, but our age. In fact we are still catching up with the notion that this is not vacationing or having a swell time. It is, and it is not. For us this is living, or the act of living the last chapters of our lives, with more purpose, meaning, and naturally, a smarter approach. Five star hotels, resorts, the best restaurants in town were never part of our quest, or zest, for living. We may have experienced something close to this. But truthfully, those experiences must have been an exception, or have been close to being free of cost. When we revisit our memories, we cannot pinpoint with precision those earlier occasions of luxury. I am glad. They must not have been that important.

At an annual Camino Gathering (American Pilgrims on the Camino) in Santa Barbara. It was meal time.

The only size backpack a pilgrim needs – as claimed by a veteran pilgrim (3x Camino Francês) at the annual Camino Gathering.

John's backpack. Typical for an average pilgrim.

3

Our Home Away From Home

I am a little pencil in the hand of a writing God
Who is sending a love letter to the world

Mother Teresa

Our home in San Miguel, the Azores, is nice by any standards, whether Portuguese, American, or Portuguese American for that matter. It is functional, spacious and nicely located; not too far from the ocean. It is sparsely furnished, but fully furnished in all aspects. The walls, all in white, which is the typical color of the land, are clutter free, dressed with a few simple paintings and some photos of the family. For certain the walls would be dressed with more pictures and frames if it were closer to our home in California. As it is, and by default, the ambiance reveals simplicity and modesty. We like it this way.

Of course money is an issue. Besides, who has loads of money to furnish another home? Certainly it has a good kitchen, and the dining area always has the flavor of *Uma Casa Portuguesa fica bem*. That means it *feels good in a Portuguese home*. We have that. Actually, the term, the title of a popular Portuguese song, alludes to feeling good in the kitchen, the center for fun and warm family chats. The kitchen is the main star setting in any family soap opera.

However, we needed another bathroom to complete the very upper floor. When the ground floor was converted to its own living quarters and rented out, a bathroom was subtracted from the whole. This is not too bad, but it is definitely an inconvenience, particularly since the home is usually full when we are there. The money we still had in San Miguel, budgeted for a few years of living, and now coupled with the new rent money, encouraged us to embark on an new undertaking – building a new bathroom.

With the assistance of our real estate friend there, a plan came to be in 2010, and the bathroom was to be built before our arrival in early April of 2011. Well, not too fast. Glitches came to the surface when the handyman contracted to do the work got trapped with identical commitments for work with his previous boss. Not even with most of the materials bought beforehand, and with money set aside and available as the work progressed, did the project come to light. Unfortunately, "remote control" from us here in US, and them there in San Miguel, does not work in such undertakings. So we were resigned, as we had limited (or no) alternatives. The building of the bathroom was placed on hold, even for longer than we thought.

This is when the old saying "God writes well through crooked lines" enters the scene. The plot changes, and the soap opera reveals new chapters, new episodes, new acts and performers. I believe this is eternally true, that God's ways come to happen where sadness turns into joy. A better and startling outcome was about to take place, and in lieu of the well planned and thought-through. Moreover, we would be the stars in the plot –living and building, the experience of construction in San Miguel. Doesn't this seem cute and refreshing? Indeed, it was.

House in San Miguel – front view

*John and Donalda enjoying a good meal at a
restaurant in Ponta Delgada (San Miguel)*

City of Ponta Delgada, San Miguel. An aspect of the shoreline boulevard.

4

The Building of a Bathroom, and Guess Who's Coming For Lunch

*To be able to feel leisure intelligently
is the last product of civilization,
And at present very few people have reached this level.*

Bertrand Russell

Once we arrived in San Miguel, we arranged a meeting with the handyman. No good excuse could comfort our disappointment. We liked, and still like, the man. After all, he had done the remodeling work and the separation of the lower quarters. We were satisfied with that work. A meeting with our real estate man revealed that another contractor was ready to do the job, in a timely manner. This time, we would take full control of the progress and stages of the work. Mestre Francisco was also known to us, for shortly after we had purchased the house in 2006 some repairs were necessary. (*Mestre* means "Master", as it relates to being an experienced tradesman.) He was the guy who did the work then. He was serious, honest and super reasonable, price-wise. He guaranteed that the job and our related needs would be taken care of in three weeks.

Donalda and I looked at each other. Could we endure three weeks of disruption, dust, and noise, and surrender ourselves like prisoners to a construction project? Was this a good plan for a vacation?

Certain dramatic and good things come to happen in one's life, and we cannot put a finger on exactly why, when, or to what purpose. If the plan for the bathroom was drawn from a need, sketched in logi-cal terms and parameters, the execution of the plan has nothing to do with one's plan to have a "vacation". True vacations – elaborate, or one of variety - are planned, and the plans, with bread-and-butter features such as dates to begin and end, the location, and so on, are common events which produce somewhat predictable outcomes.

On the other hand, some outcomes are just mind boggling. The travel magazines, the travel sections of Sunday newspapers, and the internet advertise and showcase tons of exotic experiences: safaris, mud baths, sun bathed beaches, wild parties, and the list goes on. However, for the average American, the first choices are those within our reach; not these adventures of the famous and rich. In our case, the vacation spot was practically pre-ordained – our home in San Miguel. We had been doing this for a few years; there were no surprises about the costs or how we would spend our time. Life was good there because simplicity was valuable to us. We allowed each day to unfold, perhaps with some different wrinkles, and we handled the usual chores and repetitive steps with ease. "Smell the roses" - that's what our friends say when we appear too busy, too erratic, out of spin, out of sync with ourselves. "Relax, and smell the roses." Yes, we smell them now and then, and the perfume is good, it is real.

Let's imagine whether we could sell this plan to potential vacationers: "*A dream vacation awaits you in San Miguel, Azores. Three weeks of overseeing the building of a bathroom; communing with two workers for breakfast and lunch. No dinner required, just beer before they go home. You are free to dine alone. Vacation includes helping to buy and procure of all the necessary construction materials, and to drive the workers home.*" Oh, yes, the telephone would be ringing with requests for such a delightful vacation. They would ask, When does it start? How much does it cost? But no, let's be serious.

That was on a Friday. On the following Tuesday, the work was to commence. Yes, sir, and it did on time. Mestre Francisco's promise manifested itself nicely. "Bom dia, senhor João" (Good morning, Mr. John) a familiar voice said as I opened the door after a hard knock at the door. (The door bell would need fixing or replacement.) Norberto remembered my name or knew it from his boss, Mestre Francisco. "Pedro e eu vamos fazer o trabalho." (Pedro and I are going to do the job). I remembered him from some minor work done a few years back, thus pleasantries were in order, and exchanged. Norberto, the lead guy, was ready to roll up his sleeves and get going. He knew what was at play even before setting his eyes on the site. It was a storage area on the upper floor, to be transformed into a modern bathroom.

We liked the guy right there and then, and the feeling would stay with us throughout the project. We almost rubbed our hands with pleasure. "Yes! We are going to make it in time!" we said to each other. Mestre Francisco would come later in the afternoon and review all the details. Mind you, there was no blueprint, other than a sketch of the configuration of where all the elements would come to be, the routing of all the pipes and the placement of all the pieces and fixtures. So far, so good.

But, wait - how about the hot water? Whether you are "in hot water" or not, hot water is always an issue, particularly for us American folks used to a great and uninterrupted flow of hot water. We are definitely spoiled. The European system of generating hot water with gas heated elements was (in the yesteryears of our San Miguel plumbing) the thing. If water heating tanks like we use in North-America are making their presence there now, the water boiler (water passing through the heating element) *still* is the thing in the Azores, even now. I've come to learn that America is now experimenting with this device in certain environments, such as kitchens equipped with instantaneous heated water for a faucet. No boiling tanks (our large water heaters) are needed, and this method provides a continuous flow of hot water. The drawback, in my view, is that there is never enough hot water for multiple users at the same time. It is more like "first come, first served." I guess this is not the America way.

On the other hand, we could relax about this. This bathroom would be the lucky one regarding hot water. The plumbing of the whole house – two kitchen sinks, three bathrooms – when taking into account the house and the lower quarters, would be served by one more powerful water heating device. The new bathroom would have its own dedicated and separate equipment. I imagined one of my sons and his tribe of four, demanding bribes to use the new bathroom. I will need to wait one more year to witness the reactions, when our second son and his entourage, a package of five, visit in mid-June.

Although the new bathroom was on the third floor, the very lower floor was also the stage where all the drilling would commence. No big deal, other than the fact that this floor was occupied by renters who got up later than normal in the morning. The couple, who worked together, had some odd job that meant coming home late, like two to three o'clock in the morning. They were aware of what was taking place, and we communicated with them about our plans in advance. We promised them that the loud construction noise work would only start after ten in the morning. Difficult or not, this was agreed to by all.

Our first day was coming to a close. Norberto and Pedro worked a little beyond the hour, but the little, rusty pickup truck that was used to carry the workers from their home to the job sites and then return them back, had not come yet. This truck was perhaps one of the smallest on the market, but it was used to transport everything, including five to eight people. (That's a good example of packing Portuguese sardines!) Norberto and Pedro had brought their lunch as they usually would, I suppose. I can't remember who thought of it first, Donalda or I; but our thoughts were in tandem. We said, "Okay guys, tomorrow we will cook you lunch. Have a beer before leaving." We handed them both a cold and nice local beer, and the satisfaction in their eyes was visible. They replied with sincere thanks; they were grateful to be noticed. The pickup truck finally arrived, then they were gone and we were left to our thoughts. "Not bad for a first day." They had covered a lot of territory: they had started cutting up from the corner of the rear of the house, burrowing from the bottom to the top to allow all the piping (cold, hot water, sewage and electric wiring) to be installed and connected.

The second day came. I came to expect the usual greeting "Bom dia senhor João" and I enjoyed it day after day. In fact, when I was in the kitchen preparing breakfast for Donalda and me, I would reply to either one of them without seeing their faces: "Bom Dia Norberto" or "Bom Dia, Pedro." It felt good – *senhor João* - and the fact that they were back to get the construction train moving again.

My memory of the old days as a kid flashed back. Sixty or sixty-five years is not too long ago to rewind those old times and experiences. "Respect" was a word with immense power in the relationship we had with our elders and relatives, and in the relationship one social class had with another. It was the currency that earned a good word from our parents for behaving well, it was the passport for good recommendations to anything of value in our simple lives. Let's face it - *respect* was a demanded behavior in any environment we encountered, but more important, the lack of it would be met with unwelcome consequences.

I said to Pedro and then to Norberto, "By the way, do you like American coffee?" I asked this as a way to suggest they take their first work break, American style. "Yes, why not?" said Norberto. "We know

Americans drink big *canecas* (mugs) of coffee, but it does not beat the way we drink our small cups of espresso. But sure, we will try yours." All this dialogue was in Portuguese, with its peculiarities, sounds and flavors. At 9:30am, the coffee was ready and augmented with a *bolo lêvedo* (a sort of heavy muffin that looks like an English muffin) and some cheese. *Bolo lêvedo* tastes different from an English muffin, but is good anyway. Besides, it is a treat of the island. The joy on their faces and then the gratitude of their words were real.

Lunch for that day was no surprise for us or for them: fish stew. By now, we have become good at this thing of cooking fish on the island, in the island style. Although poultry, pork and beef abound, and they are good and comparable to some extent to American meats, fish still takes first place as the staple of the island's cuisine. No, not cleaned, filleted, boneless fish. This is the real thing, whole and fresh, and it is available every day in every supermarket or fish store. You buy fresh and whole and take it from there. You can have it cut and cleaned in some way. But what for? The scraps that are cut and put aside are not wasted, and can be used in many other ways. The fish head? It is part of the stew and emanates much flavor and contains some meat. As you can see we are settled into this environment. We lived it years and years ago. We still fit now.

The lunch with the workers rolled along nicely. Good food and wine most always bring the best out in us, or at least in people of good will. It did not take long for us to know everything about Norberto's life at age thirty-four. He is married for the second time (unusual in our old times, but typical today, even for Portugal), with a child from the first marriage and an infant from the second wife. All we came to know about Norberto was his toughness, the hard times and struggles he had, but also his unwavering hope and determination. I admire the man. Despite our meal and conversation, the one-hour break for lunch was not breached. They resumed their work and progress took place right in front of our eyes. We were happy for a very fulfilling day.

The energy and raw intelligence that Norberto displayed was matched by Pedro's hard work. But this is where Pedro's strong attributes stop. There's nothing lazy about the young man, but he is twenty-one years old and acts like a teenager, still. We would, as the days progressed, witness how exasperated Norberto was by Pedro's carelessness, cluelessness and forgetfulness. Norberto would say, "Eu vou-te dar na cabeça com este tijolo; tens que aprender e não te esqueceres de nada." (*I'm going to hit your head with this brick so that you don't forget things.*) Or "corisco rapaz, eu vou-te dar uma pancada para teres mais cuidado e fazeres menos barulho." *Damn boy, I am going to hit you hard until you learn to make less noise.*) That last one was somewhat unfair, since it was imposing a temporary rule, and one that was very difficult to heed.

Donalda and I had already decided to offer lunch for the following day. We kind of took the view that they were our guests; not our workers. Most of the things we, human beings, do in later life will relate to our upbringing. Back in the old days, friends and relatives travelling from afar would stop at our homes, unannounced – no cell phones, or any phone, and not by car, but perhaps by foot or bus – around a meal time. In truth there was no set meal time, other than the noon time divided the day, and then sunset designated the evening. Whether their stop was on purpose or not the ritual was the same: "Sorry for stopping unannounced and interrupting what you're doing; we just thought of stopping by, just to say hello."

"Of course, dear," our family would quickly reply and follow their disclaimer with a nice zinger, an honest-to-God truth: "a panela que faz para dois, tambem faz para três ou quatro." The translation, meant with all its warmth says no more than: "the pot that cooks for two, most likely will serve two more." Many times it would accommodate four, or six, or even more. Hence, adding Norberto and Pedro to our lunch meal would not translate into a big ordeal. A couple of times, and to change the routine, I would go out to buy cooked food like grilled chicken, roasted pork buds, or pizza. Not a staple of the island or the country, pizza is found and cooked almost everywhere. Italian flavors, re-invented by America' mass-market cooking know-how, is now as important as the local fare. The McDonalds, the Burger Kings, the Pizza Huts and many other America's food brands are in Portugal. Starbucks coffee is not there yet; they are not used to big *canecas*. Oh, food is such a good connector of the dots in the global village. One day it may make the difference in global relations.

Norberto and Pedro enjoyed the second day of lunch and conversation, concluded with a sincere thank you. They also hinted that we did not need to do things like that to them. We understood that too. "No problem, no harm, just a pleasure" we retorted.

Early stages of bathroom preparation; breaking concrete and burrowing channels for housing the pipes.

Lunch, a fish stew, with Norberto (front) and Pedro (next)

Breaking a concrete wall to allow pipes to be housed in the burrowed space.

5

The Sub Plots

O' beware my lord, of jealousy; it is the green-eyed monster
which doth mock the meat it feeds on.

Othello, by Shakespeare

Day three, four, five and so on came, and the soap opera sustained the same flavor as on the first day of the play. We were, as we approached the final days, getting a little tired. Not with the responsibility, created by ourselves, of feeding them and us. It was just that the construction work, the progress, the little glitches, annoyances and other constraints were impacting us in some way. The routine became a job, with its elements of time, substance and purpose.

We enjoyed these moments for their hard work and purpose, but on the other hand, the stories we were discovering were of real people. There were real struggles, in the case of Norberto. We observed the growing up of Pedro; still young with a teenager's demeanor, but full of zest and a free spirit. In comparison, our lives and the lives of our sons and friends in America, even including the damage that the economic implosion inflicted on us, were much better than that of Norberto. We felt this weight in some form, and it added to our fatigue. Each lunch time we heard their admiration for our creative yet practical cooking, and we also had conversations about daily moments, trials and rewards.

The work was progressing nicely, with minor glitches and correctable problems. Anyone that is involved with major house repairs and improvements knows that what was planned in advanced is met with some unforeseen obstacles later. Many obstacles are because even well conceived ideas sometimes play out differently in the execution process. In any project there are changes and cost overruns. One even may need to cut corners or modify the final look. We reviewed our expenses as they related to our informal budget. We were there but needed to curb our impulse of upgrading unnecessarily. While Norberto and Pedro were doing work on the lower floor, other components of the job were being tackled by others: an electrician, a water heater installer and a carpenter. Meantime Mestre Luis, the carpenter and the original designated handyman, was dragging his feet on his portion of the job - the carpentry work. As much as we liked him, his patent delays were testing our patience. At least, *I* was losing some patience.

For reasons other than purely professional ones, my wife was more tolerant. Mestre Luis would come invariably at night to do some of the work. Tagging along were his wife and two kids. Good people, but all of this "inclusion" would make my day too long. The workers, the materials buying, the cooking and then three more hours of some sort of work and conversational engagement became the straw that broke the camel's back. I was less patient. This lack of patience was also triggered by Mestre Luis' habitual nitpicking that Norberto was missing something here and there, or in clear terms criticizing his overall work. I was tired of the unsolicited criticism, but then I was reminded by my godson, Paulo, who helped along the way in so many ways, that this behavior is typical in Portugal. Perhaps it is likewise elsewhere, but the thought then was about the professionals on the island. In simple terms, when more than one professional is involved in an undertaking, it is common that one will criticize the other and so on. The plot thickens, and then the fun stops. These are human frailties at play.

Trust me, besides his hard work, Norberto was very smart. Although the Portuguese have made great strides towards 100% literacy and a great majority receives secondary education, somehow Norberto missed the boat or fell through the cracks, perhaps because he needed to make a living at a very tender age. His education did not go beyond the first year of school. He could read a little, but writing was out in left field. Yet his brain was sharp and his excellent memory was his support, his crutch. Take as an example that most houses – frame and walls - are built with concrete blocks. Walls are drilled and burrowed to fit all the plumbing pipes, in the proper directions. The large quantity and variety of pipes and accessories must be tallied correctly.

I would observe Norberto, his eyes studying the house, up and down, right and left, and his lips rattling off the types, the sizes, dimensions, quantities of all the materials to Pedro. Then, in my company, he would review all the numbers with the hardware folks, revise something here or there as his eyes and fingers touched the materials and his brain was recalculating, re-computing or correcting his previous exercise. Fantastic was my conclusion. The guy is good, he has brains.

Norberto would say, *Oh Senhor João, você tem um serrote eléctrico?* (Oh Mr. John do you have a power saw*?) Tem uma luz de extensão?* (Do you have an extension cord with a light?) *E uma espátula grande ou média?* (How about a medium size or big spatula?) These and many others of their ongoing requests became part of my collection of phrases I would laugh about later. I thought, my home is in California, I am here in San Miguel, and you're asking me for tools? Are you kidding? Why would they expect I would have these tools?

Norberto and Pedro could have played the roles of Abbott and Costello. (Almost, for both were skinny and of normal build. Norberto was short, about my height, and Pedro much taller.) Of course these guys are not comedians or actors. I bet they could not make people laugh if they actually wanted to. Yet their daily routine was full of humorous morsels. If these moments were arranged together they could be funny scripts to be used by standup comedians. Their dialogues and graphic gestures about their work routine had flavors of their own making.

This issue of the tools, though, was a reminder that even in this modern world, and the Azores have not been left behind, many a worker still operates with just the minimum of tools. Without a doubt the job required the use of some modern tools that are more powerful and efficient. However these were borrowed or shared from job to job routinely. A call for a certain tool would take place and there it came from another job site. But some other and equally important tools, the ones you would carry in a tool box, were not in sight or on the site. Whatever Norberto or Pedro needed, beyond their meager assembly of mandatory tools, had to be sourced from my own limited inventory or I would have to buy them. In America, the average, credible mason would have a normal tool bucket wrapped around by a very well organized leather tool apron. Carpenters and others would be equipped with impressive tool boxes and state of the art power tools. I am certain many in S. Miguel do have them. In fact, the electrician and the carpenter did equip themselves with nice, useful tool boxes.

Since Norberto did not have such large assortment of tools, creativity was brought into play many a time. For instance, rather than using a professional blow torch like plumbers use in their trade, Norberto would simple use a piece of newspaper, light a match to it and burn the edges of the PVC pipes, melting the plastic to make the connectors of elbows, tees and other accessories fit together. PVC glue was used there too, for other applications, including in the whole assemble of pipes and fittings, but for strange reasons or because of the pipe's properties, pipes of five or six inches in diameter normally connect to each other by way of heat, softening their connection. For sure, each day brought new revelations and creative undertakings.

A note about *mestres,* or small time mom and pop contractors. Mestre Francisco continued to impress me beyond any measure. He provided very fair pricing, and straight forward explanations about the job. His honest recommendations, or just confirmations of value of one material, one item, one appliance, cannot be ignored. There is no varnish, no bullshitting, or any inference that he tried to gain in some measurable way by his answers. What you see and what you get is unequivocally good, fair and honest.

Normally many of us find opportunities to bargain about a purchase price or job cost quote. In fact, I am used to applying this technique to any big purchase or service contract in America. It is in my blood, and my brain recognizes that the first price is rarely the correct price. Whether our culture instills this in us, compels us, or educates us to shop around for a better product and a better price, the same approach is utilized. I utilize it frequently, with any need that calls to be fulfilled.

Yet when it came to Mestre Francisco's pricing of his services or a specific project, the only phrase I added was: "Are you sure this is it? How about cost overruns, unforeseen situations?" His answers were complete and to the point: "Senhor João, I calculated this well and do not anticipate any surprises to take place." I would look at him, incredulous, which would trigger a follow-up answer. "If the unforeseen comes to happen, we both will talk about it and deal with it responsibly." That's it – the end of the story. Indeed, in the end there were modifications, mostly from me, that would need adjustments. But never anything that compromised or betrayed his word. Even a money gift for him and his wife was reluctantly accepted. I like the man; I wish he were in America.

Norberto and Pedro's job was about finished on the thirteenth day.

Donalda and I were happy with the results, even though the other small jobs belonging to the carpenter and the electrician were to be done. They had cleaned their tools and gathered their stuff up right at the end of the day and they were ready to wait for their buddies to pick them up. We were prepared to say good-bye, and to reward them in some measurable way – money and wine as gifts – but we were emotionally sad to say farewell. Needless to say, all of us had tears in our eyes. Even the free spirited Pedro showed unexpected emotion. Life is good when simplicity, respect and love are all at the same table. We learned it well.

The days that followed were no picnic. I had to do some serious thinking about my pilgrimage. The cleaning of the construction mess left behind, even with the help of our cleaning lady for a couple days, and then to prepare and ready the house for our soon-to-arrive English guests and friends occupied our attention. Yet I could not help but rewind the clock again a little bit to the recent experience with our construction project. Many images, like revisiting pictures in slow motion, made me laugh out loud, just by myself.

Finished bathroom – view of entrance, mirror over the lavatory

Finished bathroom – shower, bidet, toilet and lavatory

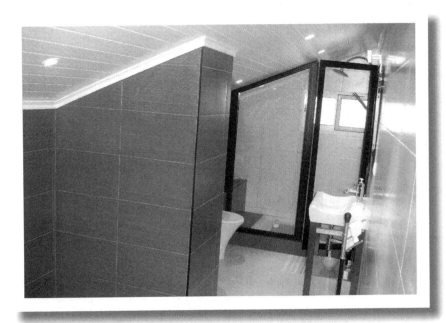

Another view of the bathroom – shower stall at the end

6

Our Guests From England

For I, who hold sage Homer's rule the best,
Welcome the coming, speed the going guest

Alexander Pope

The bathroom – the finished product – was nearing completion. For all intents and purposes it was ready to be used. The floor, the walls, the ceiling, the lights, the shower stall and all the more functional pieces – toilet, bidet, water basin – all lined up nicely. It was like an orchestra with all the players and their instruments cleverly assembled and ready to produce harmonious and beautiful sounds. An excellent orchestra requires all the necessary instruments; in some cases duplicate instruments and more dramatic pieces. It must, if it aims to produce sounds of immense effect. An orchestra with fewer of the same type of instrument – like one less violin or clarinet – could still produce great sounds and would likely make me content; I might not be able tell the difference. Anyway, what do I know about music?

But our bathroom would not disappoint anyone. In spite of certain glitches such as the floor design being different than the one we originally planned, Donalda and I liked what we saw. The unfinished business was minor and belonged to our ever-procrastinating carpenter. Making the final and un-required inspection, Donalda and I counted our blessings for reaching the end in spite of our divergent tastes and stubborn opinions. We did it; what a miracle. But kidding aside, our bathroom was done one week before the Gassnners - our friends from England - would arrive. We experienced relief of all sorts and felt rewarded for all the efforts around the construction work. What we thought very early on to be possible, then later on aborted, and then resurrected almost from the blue sky (or let's give due credit, from above), was now behind us.

The Gassnners, and we too, regretted that they could not come during the biggest festival in San Miguel, as well in the Azores. SATA International's (the local Azorean airlines) flights between England and San Miguel were from Sunday to Sunday. Changes and connections through Lisbon were possible, but the price tag would be measurably different. Besides, our calendar of other commitments, like my own planned departure in just days for my pilgrimage, made the festival wish not doable. They would participate in part of the celebrations, with the exception of the big enchilada – the Sunday procession. This one event would be missed. Actually their return home would be on that same Sunday morning.

The Gassnners live and have lived in Swindon, England, forever. We came to know them through our sons Victor and Tony. The Gassnner's son Paul met Victor at an international soccer tournament for Catholic schools in Burgos, Spain. From that moment on, Paul and Victor began building a friendship which kept being fertilized in many ways. Years later the friendship baton got passed to their brothers - Tony on Victor's side and Matt on Paul's side. In 1994, Victor, and then in 2002, Tony, went to England following their college graduation. As the years progressed, visits and reciprocation of visits continued with all four, particularly on their weddings.

I visited both Victor (1994) and Tony (2002) in England and thereby met the Gassnners as well. Carlos accompanied me on the trip of 2002. And so we have a new set of friends. I guess, in our times of global reach or global village relationships, this is not news. Thank God, for here is more hope that we, citizens of the planet, will find more ways to co-exist. It is unfortunate that this idea of a global village does not have bigger traction. Wars still exist, disagreements and disputes abound, and distrust is on the menu of the day.

We didn't know whether one week would be enough for two couples to find common ground, enjoyment, camaraderie, mutual tastes and desires, but it appears this one week did the job. Matt, their youngest son, had spent a few days with us there two years before, and did not dissuade them from paying a visit to us as well, and to discover the wonders of these islands with visible volcanic origins; its people and their hospitality. It is not a prescription for togetherness, but both the Gassnners and we are Catholic. Mike and Teresa are about our age, retired, and perhaps re-enacting the spark that brought them together. Their children reflect their successful parenting efforts, thus they manifest a stress free atmosphere of tranquility.

We only visit San Francisco, just less than an hour away from our home in San Ramon, when guests are in town. Like San Francisco, which was our first home in the United States, the scenic, gorgeous natural parts of S. Miguel are good to visit with guests. So it was that we took the Gassnners to most places of interest in San Miguel. The Azores are composed of nine islands; England is also an island. You might think the similarity ends right there, for the population of the Azores is about a quarter million inhabitants, and London just by itself is more populous than the Azores and the mainland of Portugal together.

There are however more similarities. San Miguel is always green, like in England, which means it must rain regularly. Overcast mornings, the occasional drizzle, the sun-teasing afternoons, like a game of hide and seek between balmy sun and bold, large clouds rolling over the immense Atlantic, were companions in our car trips. All of these elements were familiar to our English guests. Not a big deal. No prayer for Caribbean or Algarve type weather was not heard. The higher above, whether busy with other more pressing of the world's needs and problems, knew better. Mountains and valleys, meadows, pastures and plenty of deep ocean surrounds the abundant steep coastline. Natural and profound beauty was on display every single day. And reality, being truer than fantasy, continues to claim that beauty is found in the eyes of the beholder. Well, the Azores do possess that beauty and the Gassnners loved and enjoyed it.

Surprises of a different kind do happen every now and then. On one of those get-out-of-the-house-and-visit-the-city things, we were met with a pleasant surprise, at least for both Donalda and me. One of my half brothers and his wife were strolling around the attractive shoreline boulevard, and we spotted them as we were driving home. Definitely many Americans and Canadians of Portuguese descent can be found at one time or another visiting their birth place. Aristides, my half brother, who lives in Brampton, a large suburb of Toronto, and I rarely see each other. And like many other folks and family members we know, we also take trips that the other knows little or nothing about. This is normal. Then, if we come across some folks we know from America or Canada, the adrenalin of the moment is palpable. In fact, every year that we are there we end up by coming across folks we know in US. Those are opportunities for great joy. Naturally the rest of the day was spent together, and with the Gassnners. It became a pleasant surprise for them as well.

Our guests left and the big festival celebrations continued. This evoked the old times when we, as kids, would love the chance to be let loose and free, to chase a girl here or there or have lots of fun with our friends. In a few more days and my trip to Continental Portugal and Spain would be on my calendar. Not bad. I was looking forward to the next events to take place.

The Gassnners arriving at Ponta Delgada (San Miguel) airport.

John and Donalda with brother Aristides and sister-in-law Filomena, in San Miguel

Taking the Gassnners around the island and stopping at friends – top row (l-r) Jose Linhares, Mike Gassnner, John. Lower row – Teresa Gassnner, Donalda and Maria Inez Linhares

*Sete Cidades Lake in San Miguel. One of many
of natural beauties of the island.*

Scenic view of part of another beautiful village – "Povoação".

7

Wherever There are Human Beings There are (Economic) Inequalities

It is not only that there are sharks and sardines,
lambs and wolves, weeds and grains
or that the world is what it is.

-My view

Let it be earth and God made the earth. Let it be the earth with land and water, plants and seeds, mountains and plains, peaks and valleys; with day and night; with sun and stars; and all kinds of living creatures. And God saw it was all good. And let's also have men and women, or (in simple talk), human beings. Oh, the first sin just had to happen. Thus human beings became human beings.

The less than two hour air flight from Ponta Delgada to Lisbon was not long enough to start on reading a new book or any book for that matter. After all, soon after I would arrive in Lisbon, my good friend Sá, as usual, would pick me up at the airport so I could join our friend Viegas and then proceed on our train ride from Lisbon to Leon, Spain, via Madrid. In between the plane arrival and train ride we would have only time for warm hugs, small chat, and a quick dinner. I was in no mood to read. My mind naturally drifted to Donalda, who would stay behind, alone for sixteen days, in San Miguel. Not a comfortable thought.

Staying behind was not a first time occurrence. At least two or three times in the past we were separated for periods of one week, to four, to eight. Neither of us liked the idea, but with her still engaged in full time work and me with freedom to spare, it became a point that one needed to do what needed to do. Protected and distracted by her job, surrounded by three sons, daughters in law and a bunch of grandkids, it would make the pain of separation less stressful. Indeed all were part of her support system. This time was different: she would stay alone in a known environment, but remote and away from her comfort zone and family support. Our friends there, great as they were, would not be enough. I felt pained at the idea.

As the plane moved across the Atlantic on its one thousand mile journey, after the usual snacks provided by the airline, new thoughts about old things and recent matters replaced the thoughts about Donalda. There is too much agony, misery, and economic distress in the world for it not to occupy one's mind at every turn. It is not only in America, my country, my home, but also in Portugal, my birth place and my second home. The world, as I view it, or as many people of intelligence also view it, is in a mess. The mess has always existed, whether in small doses or nicely camouflaged.

But this time there was no tiptoeing, sweet talking or dancing around it. No matter how much the politicians sugar-coated their messages, pointed fingers at their neighbors instead of themselves, lived in denial or promised pinpointed solutions of their own, the mess was more than real. For my generation who did not experience the Depression, and the generations of my sons and grand kids that follow, the mess stunk. And this time, at least there would be enough shit for a fan to be occupied in spreading immense scent to a wider radius and audience. The funny part was that this thought, replacing the more romantic thoughts of Donalda of just a few moments back, started me thinking of Norberto.

No, I was not in love with Norberto. I had just absorbed his situation, juxtaposed it to the situation of other people, and felt sick about what a bunch of privileged human beings had done to a great number of others. It is unfair, inhuman, just plain sick. No wonder the sit-ins at Wall Street and beyond came to be part of the daily news events. Whether I agree or not with the Occupy protestors is not the point. The point is that people were betrayed; and turnaround solutions cannot be found, and Wall Street does not care - or is simply brain dead.

Donalda and I were affected by the financial collapse of 2007 -08. Forget the home values, as far as we were concerned. After all we were not selling our home. Our retirement savings, progressively and methodically built through our working years, was a serious concern, for they received an unnecessary punch. Granted, we could have been more prudent or fearful of collapses. Yet previous recessionary periods had taught us something of value. We thought we had done our homework. Millions and millions more had thought the same, so we were not alone. This is no comfort for any of us caught in the web of lies, incompetence and greed. The reality and the inevitable conclusion that the market, Wall Street as a whole, is infected with sharks and snakes alike slowly and surely came to strike at us, at our heads and pockets.

Late 2009 and most of 2010 brought some market relief, which allowed us to refill some of our two 401k baskets. Although still not reaching the earlier levels, the refilling was restoring some hope. This ride would continue, but with erratic stalls, such as the news on the country of Greece. Ireland had already tanked, Portugal was also on life support, and smoke was coming with a Spanish scent. The market makers were again playing their game of yo-yo. A flash back to my professional years in banking surfaced; it was a memory of one of the many seminars I attended. This one was about a theory, with an example of Swiss cheese, which always made me chuckle, whether with the humorous parts of the theory or because it actually makes sense in real life's exchanges. The money changers or big time handlers, with their maniac concoctions, presented most of us – practical investors on our own, via 401ks, mutual funds, pension plans – with an appetizing platter of Swiss cheese. At the end of the wild party, once the fire erupted, they kept the cheese and we, of course we, got the **holes.** No wonder the OWS (Occupy Wall Street) movement has gotten nothing but thin air.

Norberto, with basically not much to his name, with just his small income from paycheck to paycheck, would survive. After all, he was used to living with less. But the outcome was still miserable and harsh. Even with his professional credentials of a mason and everything else related, such as hard work and good traits, would not be enough to ensure steady employment. America was in a mess; Europe, through the smaller countries, was quickly getting smelly from the symptoms of economic and financial diarrhea. In the case of Portugal, with no room to sneak through or better yet to hide, obscurity became impossible. It took years for Porto wine, or perhaps a decade for Mateus or Lancers Rosé, to educate Americans about the pleasing flavors of aperitif wine, thus creating some positive notoriety for the name of Portugal. Then the financial mess accomplished the exact opposite propaganda objectives in practically no time. For two years, and it is still ongoing, the name Portugal, together with the names of Greece, Iceland, Ireland, and the larger Europe's peripheral neighbors, became synonymous with "economic futility".

"Made in America" brands had been for two decades slowly replaced by "Made in Japan," or "Made in Singapore," or "Made in Taiwan" or "Made in Mexico." As the century turned, these gave way to "Made in China." But America was not finished with our "Made in America" fever. Are you kidding? Giving up our "know-how" of anything, our leadership? We always reinvented ourselves with freshly minted new products and ideas. If old industry products were no longer competitive because of copycats and were manufactured cheaper elsewhere, something new always emerged from the USA creative machine. It was a given, our destiny to find something new to replace the old. This time, with the dot.com phenomenon imploding at the turn of the century, it was being replaced with a more dramatic phenomenon – the social media. America credibility was restored again in grand fashion. Unfortunately this new "Made in America" idea, as it related to the money changers, was not good enough. It was clean, legitimate and restricted to and led by Silicon Valley and related companies. It was not under the exclusive domain or short reach of the money changers. If by all accounts this was economically good for America, it would be of a lesser value to Wall Street.

You see, Wall Street always prided itself (erroneously) for being the economic engine of America, the generator of wealth and jobs. Unfortunately they generate over fifty percent of the profits, but only twelve percent of our economic value. The difference travels into the pockets of the money changers. Of course they could also be doing God's work; as claimed by Lloyd Blankfein, Chairman of Goldman Sachs. The new economy was not good enough for them. So a new export innovation, courtesy of Wall Street, in the works for two decades, was ready to take center stage in the whole planet. Wall Street's savvy, in the form of innovative investment products and strategies, or in street language, "investment crap," was ready for the final act. Yes, Wall Street was ready to proudly hoist the America flag again as the dominant player in the world. The "Made in America" thing, the brand being perfected with artistic skill, was equally and flawlessly being peddled to the countries named previously, who eagerly and gratefully bought them. Yes, everyone in addition to the Americans would become very rich overnight. The fruits of capitalism would be no longer just a privilege of the Americans, but extended to the rest of the world.

We are great sellers of snake oil, and equally skilled at finding incompetent, or better yet willing, suckers. The victims of Enrons, Tycos, Global Crossings and the like in early 2000 were not enough of a lesson. Shame on us. That Bernie Madoff cheated many of his friends and acquaintances with gusto is understandable. Most of them were acquaintances, after all, and most pushed their way into his circle of quick money makers. That they had money to lose did not hurt a bit. It actually reinforced Bernie's indifference. That's not fair, but at least they all had money to lose. But countries? Practically a whole continent? Even the stronger countries in Europe (Germany, Sweden, Finland, Norway, Belgium and a few more) cannot escape the spillover from the collapse of any one of their weaker siblings. Remember the fan working all day and night, spreading the scent of manure?

Really, I was not that aggravated on my two hour plane trip. Not even as disgusted as I became during the few months in 2008 as I witnessed the financial and investments domino game unfolding with incredible speed. Just compare it with a tennis match or the Wimbledon finals, featuring the best tennis players. Your head turns left and right as the balls are volleyed with astronomic speed. Our financial headache lasted, long beyond the time a tennis match is played out. And then it subsided, because we became virtually certain that we could do nothing constructive to correct the course. Letting things take their course was a less damaging course of action. At least for us it was. The games Wall Street play are too fast, with a ton of variations.

Norberto would survive, for he is used to not having much. Others would survive too. Yet, many others, on both sides of the Atlantic, would deny their fate, resist the change. And all would eventually become resigned to the fact that this was a bad dream – and that no certain and exact way to be rich ever existed. The crooked way, yes. One will have to settle with being poor or live with less. And the rich, of course will get richer. It is a given. No problem here. Having some bread crumbs left over from their tables perhaps should be enough; enough for the rest of us. Thus the reappearance of *third world* style and living conditions are becoming almost a reality. I do not like it, but unfortunately I see it coming in some parts of Europe, with some reach into America, too.

After I allowed these thoughts to occupy me too much for too long, I turned my mind to my approaching pilgrimage. I was certain of my need to have some sort of mind cleansing. The pilgrimage would oblige, and had the ingredients to cause that to happen. I needed to be away from the negative news, from the repetitive blame game, the convenient denial and the ineptitude of those in power, those in charge of recapturing the people's hopes. Greed, fraud and rewarded incompetence will always be with us. Wherever there are human beings these outcomes will always be with us. Still, for God's sake - not to this great extent, this great magnitude and worldwide reach. People need to hope that there are human beings of good standing, good heart, strong will and undeniable desire to give it all they have for the betterment of us all, yes all, human beings.

The time to arrive at Portela Airport in Lisbon was approaching. I was happy and regaining my serenity. The less than positive thoughts were vanishing; being correctly replaced by thoughts and feelings of hope. Hope that God will provide. I also counted my blessings for being able to afford these trips. Always economically, and the cheapest possible way, but clearly my situation was better compared to some others. I could do and I am doing these activities. At seventy, my health is not bad. If on one hand, my body or my health could be described as a broken vase glued with the best "crazy" glue, on the other hand I am okay, health-wise. I have ailments of various types, perhaps because of my genes or acquired with aging. But I still can move along well and undertake projects that normally would be more suited for a younger body or mind. So, I am lucky and thank God as often as God talks to me. The plane circles around and over the top of Lisbon. The topography is different of that of other big cities. And I like it. It is my Lisbon, or in Portuguese it is my *Lisboa*.

As I thought, Sá, his wife and Viegas were waiting for me at the airport. It is always nice to see these folks, friends of many years. Viegas is ready to have a bite and take aim at the train station. His backpack is ready while my supplies are mixed in my duffel bag with other clothing items, ones I will need eventually when the pilgrimage is over. As part of the plan, Donalda will rendezvous with me in Santiago at the end of the pilgrimage. Fortunately Sá's home is not far either from the airport or from the train station. It all worked well, even if I annoyed them for not being backpack-ready. Why worry?, I thought. The ugly and miserable thoughts I held during the flight were now old history.

So I let the simple aspects of life take over and refresh my soul. Indeed they did.

Yet in the end, to wrap up this chapter's title, I cannot resist my need to liberate myself about the view of the whole economic mess. The lesson I have learned rests with this conclusion: ***Not only are all segments of society hurt, but the economy as a whole loses real traction if inequalities are present, or stubbornly kept alive, by those wielding too much economic power.*** Let the tide rise for all, unless you are prepared to be kicked in the butt. Not everyone is.

A typical pilgrim couple crossing a small village.

8

The Camino Pilgrimage

For Mercy has a human heart;
Pity, a human face;
And Love, the human form divine;
And Peace, the human dress.

William Blake, Songs of Innocence

No denying that the *Camino* experience of 2008 had instilled in me, and Viegas in some manner, the urgency to get it done again in 2011. Yet it was hard to gauge Viegas's readiness in early 2011. He was over seven thousand miles away in Portugal. He is well read and knowledgeable, with excellent observations, but he was the eternal *mañana* kid when writing. Prior to the Internet and the more economic telephone calling plans, writing was by far the most logical method of communicating for long and varied personal news and information. With Viegas , only the telephone – at Christmas or special occasions - did the trick. As opposed to Sá, who always engaged in nice and useful dialogues, Viegas was the consummate *Alentejano,* he felt that tomorrow, or never, was just fine. Let's be necessarily honest here: *Alentejanos* (natives of Alentejo province) more than any other folks in Portugal, receive a bum rap when it comes to siesta, or any exhibition of the "leave it for tomorrow" thing. The region of Alentejo – the geography, its people, its genuine honesty and intellect – is one that I am proud to know about. If jokes of the "the dumb blonde" type are attributed to *Alentejanos* it is only because we, of Portuguese descent, are jealous of them. Great region, great people.

But anyway, back to Viegas. In today's advanced world, Viegas and I occasionally resorted to the telephone. The occasional brief telephone conversations via Skype only revealed scant information on how much he was ready - physical readiness, emotional, and the other inner feelings that surpass the fear of the unknown. The vagueness of his answers could indicate some sort of sand-bagging me, like he did in 2008, but I also knew he was superstitious and feared that something weird could happen; this would dissolve his emotional investment in this pilgrimage. Unfortunately it did. A bad outcome almost at the mid point of the pilgrimage, did floor him. So even before we started, secrecy, or toning down the expectations of the undertaking, was his *modus operandi*. I understood that.

Viegas was excited and ready. My plane trip ticket to Lisbon had been purchased at least for a week. So, no change there. However, our train trip to Leon had been planned for the following morning after my arrival in Lisbon. A problem – a railway workers strike being advertised and staged for Friday, the day of our train departure – turned into a welcome opportunity to take the train shortly after my arrival in Lisbon. Turning problems into opportunities had been for a long time part of my professional life and career. So it was that the workers' strike problem offered us an opportunity to start our way one day earlier and perhaps allow ourselves more time to make some sort of bold alterations to our pilgrimage itinerary. This thinking was indicative of old folks like ourselves who are either relaxing on life's later days, or who jump with joy for finding little, insignificant opportunities to make up for lost time. A savings of one day in the program was such an incentive to add another new twist. We are in many instances anxious to save a minute here and there and to recapture what we just can't have anymore. It is a nice rut we find ourselves, but a rut nevertheless. No wonder that I find older people always in a hurry, sneaking here and there or impatient at the checker's line. On the other hand, I may find them totally absent minded; oblivious that the world is populated by people other than themselves. Viegas and I play this role well. We have credentials to the old folks club.

So, with Sá's intervention, again the train trip changed and we were on our way, saying goodbye to our world of known and familiar comforts and apparent normalcy and immersing ourselves in the world of drift and make do with what you have. I badly needed this world – it is far from being homeless, and yet far from being normal, comfortable, at home.

The stretch from Lisbon to Madrid was done on a normal train. Not a "fast" train, but not nearly as slow as WW II trains. This was a "red eye" trip, beginning at ten thirty in the evening and in second class. That means the next eight hours lay ahead – comfortless. The train was not crowded, we had a whole row of seats for ourselves, but no space to make the bench a real bed. Each row had space for three but no room to stretch. Each seat in the row was individually manufactured with padded (I guess with steel in them) arm rests dividing each space. This is bad business; some sort of devious plan had been devised to create discomfort for passengers in a deserted train. A couple of trips to the bar, a beer and a cappuccino, made the trip less long. Yet many hours remained; sleep was invited to be part of the game. No bed, bad seats, no space, and the trip became more of a test than a comfort. I wished the railway strikers had not triggered such an uncomfortable outcome. I guess Viegas slept okay or found a way to endure the train with no apparent side effects. I was happy for this signaled to me that the pilgrimage would be a breeze. How wrong I came to be.

We arrived in Madrid. I cannot remember the station's name (there are a few), and we found ourselves already pilgrimage fit. As usual Viegas leaned on me for the most basic stuff. Perhaps it was his *Alentejano* habits, his diminished hearing capacity, or just the fact I am more used to taking charge. Viegas's habit of asking me for everything - café, restrooms, and information booths -started to build its own nest. This would eventually take on a whole dimension as our real walk got underway. This role, like it is my destiny to be responsible for others, could not be left behind in my other everyday world. A pilgrimage or a trip alone, of any kind, would free one (or me) from being responsible for someone else. But like old times, Viegas would become like a fly clinging to me, as an abalone clings to a rock.

That train station was as big as a typical mid size airport terminal. The station, with an ambiance of a shopping mall, does provide opportunities for the locals to have a good night out. "Hey, honey, let's spend some time at the train station." "Doing what?" "Just see and enjoy a nice train station. Why not?" The espressos are good, the stores sell stuff and one can imagine taking a trip. Yes, a virtual trip with a station and trains.

The stretch from Madrid to Leon was another story, a better one, with modern and faster trains and with the proper ambiance. For starters it was a nine thirty in the morning trip, on a well traveled railway corridor. The carriages – all of them – were full, with seats properly assigned (yes we sat on the correct numbered seats, but in the wrong carriage) with comfort to spare. The two and one half hours trip zipped through the northern plains of Spain very nicely. We forgot about the time and then we, rather quickly, found ourselves in Leon, ready for the start of our odyssey. As opposed to our walk in 2008, when we chose a cab to take us from the train station to Porto's cathedral as the beginning of our journey, this time we decided to walk from the station to the *albergue*. (inn or hostel) Somehow, without thinking, our mood was for a true, Spartan style pilgrimage. No such luxury – a taxi – was contemplated.

It took several approaches to Leon natives (we assumed) to ask for and receive directions to the albergue. Leon is a good size city, not everyone knows everyone. We thought *Camino* Santiago is as common as taking siesta in Spain. Everyone has a siesta so everyone, we surmise, should be an expert on everything around it. After all the albergue, together with the grueling walking, is the most important external component of a pilgrimage. It is not like back home, when the male (chauvinist), confronted with a need for driving directions, is reluctant to ask for such un-male things. I guess GPS gadgets were created for stubborn males, and some brain-reduced women. Most certainly it was made for me. Of course, I am revealing my *mea culpa,* too.

We did circumnavigate our way from the train station to the albergue well. It took longer by half of the time, but we got there just in time to get an acceptable bunk bed. We calculated, as we were moved through the aisles of the army barracks, that the albergue, with its one hundred sixty beds, would not take long to get full. It being my first day, and I still fresh, untested yet, I thought I could sleep on the floor and sell my spot for a profit. When you are tired and there is no room at the Inn, one will pay anything.

Viegas was feeling good and motivated. It was a good sign and a relief for me. Just congregating with lots of people from different backgrounds and regions of the world, I could sense, was exciting him. After registration, which took some time, for the line was long (and perhaps fast approaching the moment that "we are full, no more room,") we were ready for dinner. A group of Koreans folks with colorful Korean paraphernalia –flags, head bands, ski poles, and backpacks - were having the time of their lives. I do not know if Leon was their starting point or if they were already on their third leg of their pilgrimage. The Koreans were happy. Viegas noted this fact, and it was a sign that full communion with the pilgrimage was slowly taking shape.

After disposing of our precious luggage – our backpacks - we went out for a walk and for some chow. Instead, not far away from the albergue, we came across a convenience store where we stocked ourselves with food for the night and the following morning. It was imperative to be prepared.

The day was about to be done. It was a decent and hopeful start, for sure.

Not all walkers (pilgrims) take backpacks. Carry-
ons are also welcomed. Actually this pilgrim carried
for both. His wife (not shown) was backpack-less.

9

Beginning the Camino Walk

It gives me a deep comforting sense that things seen are temporal
And things unseen are eternal

Helen Keller

It was only on the third day of the pilgrimage that I thought of writing some notes. The desire for this pilgrimage did not come from any specific ulterior motives or visions of something very special or unique. Plain vanilla outcomes would be just fine. I just wanted to experience everything about the pilgrimage and document it in my soul. Even the pictures I planned to take were few and infrequent - only the most necessary of notes and images. I figured, if the pilgrimage turned out to be that important and dramatic, my soul and my brain would be sufficient to provide the material for later story writing.

As the pilgrimage evolved from stage to stage, and later on when Viegas aborted his participation after the fifth stage because of a serious foot problem, my note taking became a daily occurrence. Viegas's situation affected him tremendously, and it did not sit right with me either. This trip, like the one we had taken in 2008, ranked high as personal accomplishments to us. To him, I came to learn, getting an invitation for such undertaking with me was the ultimate respect for who he was. Even, when in 2008, Sá had warned me that Viegas's heart condition required monitoring and that chances were he would decline my invitation, Viegas said and proved otherwise. With a gadget to monitor his heartbeat at any given time, we adjusted our walking pace to conform to the recommendations of the gadget.

We both had invested a great portion of our friendship into this walk beyond the typical purposes of the average pilgrim. Each one of us has our own inner trips, thoughts, values and reasons for doing what we do. Viegas, a Catholic by birth and family tradition, was far from being a practicing Catholic. In fact he had some serious doubts about the value of the Church in today's environment. He is God fearing and a believer, but the Church was another story. His respect and reverence for my beliefs were of the highest order. That in itself became a bond that transcends many beliefs and obstacles. This pilgrimage was by no means the Super Bowl of important undertakings in his life. But it was close.

Nowadays almost everybody has written about the *Camino* (way, route, path). Some document it with fragmented notes and recordings, others in a diary format. Most of these writings will never be published, will be instead used for later reading or left behind for friends, as part of family legacies. The Shirley MacLaines, or the other many authors, had their reasons to document their experiences of the *Camino*. I do not know what Shirley MacLaine had in mind for doing the *Camino* or writing about it. As a Hollywood star and one who is a perpetual searcher for spiritual fulfillment, the occult, and the unknown, the reasons would be obvious: "what I learned and what I believe now." One conclusion I arrived at was that the many and varied answers from all who have done the *Camino* is it became relevant, in the end, only if one found some need to change some aspect of his or her life. That means the *Camino* made a difference in their lives. Otherwise it was only an exercise of fulfilled curiosity. Nothing wrong with that or with the results; just a sincere observation.

Before 2008 I had read about the *Camino* from Susan Alcorn, a retired teacher, who with her husband had been avid walkers on the many trails in California. They still are. Eventually the *Camino* attracted them, for the trails were good arenas for their trail walking experiences and vocation. Although her book was easy to read and did provide some help, I was still green on pilgrimages of the kind and my first walk was preceded by tons of trepidation and fear of the unknown. If age – at the time I was sixty-eight – does argue for caution, it also inspires your curiosity to do something never tried and tested. What would I lose? Now three years later and having read a few more books and comprehensive guides on the *Camino*, with one more *Camino* done, I feel more confident to record a few bits of my experiences in print format; even if only one reader – me – happens to read my notes.

I do not intend to narrate the whole essence of the trip. It was too rich and important to me so that a paragraph or a chapter or two would not do justice. At the least, if I am going to relive these beautiful and fulfilling moments, I had better do the story right. Thus what follows are just subtle recollections with the flavorful details, and the more fundamental experiences are left for another time and writing project. Indeed, I would like to do that.

One of many reminders on the Camino Frances
- a statue of a yester-centuries pilgrim.

10

A Brief Note on the Caminos

Do no dishonor to the earth lest you dishonor the spirit of man.

Henry Beston

Our pilgrimage to Santiago via the *Camino Portugués* in 2008 was as demanding as any other *Camino* walk; including the one we planned for 2011, which we found ourselves ready to get immersed in. The *Camino Frances* is the mother of all *Caminos*, or in loose *Camino* lingo, is the whole enchilada. In fact, of all the official routes to Santiago, and there are twelve of them, all with the exception of *Camino Portugués* and *Camino Aragonés* merge, at one point or another, onto the *Camino Francés*.

The *Camino Portugués*, with Lisbon as the official starting point, rarely attracts pilgrims except the long course walkers who invariably spend months on the road. The lack of hostels on the route to Porto, up north of Portugal, and the poorly marked itineraries, trails and byways make it less appealing for the typical pilgrim to start in Lisbon. Porto as a starting point is more popular, for the route from there until Santiago is shorter – only 240km – and supported by a minimum number of hostels, and the way marks are very reliable. The long course walkers I mention above are practically pros who have the stamina and temperament to endure anything in any conditions and at any season of the year. I did come across at least two of these folks who logged thousands of kilometers in months on any *Camino* or combinations of *Caminos*. Mind boggling, but very true. Why one would do such thing? The answers normally are not very clear. However one can surmise that a common reason is the "*Camino* fever."

A little less than ninety percent travel the *Camino Francés*. Because of the many starting points from the various routes leading onto the

Camino Francés, the number of pilgrims swells once the *Camino* mergers take place. The more I learn about the many aspects of the *Camino* the more I come to recognize that for all intents and purposes the *Camino Francés* starts at St. Jean Pied de Port, in southwest France. The next stage starting point, Roncesvalles, now in Spanish territory, equally attracts many pilgrims. From there on, and after crossing the Pyrenees, the breathtaking conquest, all options open up, including starts at various points of the route. Eight hundred kilometers later, and with the calendar marking thirty to forty days, we are in Santiago.

The differences on the various *Camino's* popularities are obvious. Yet, all combine the elements of spiritual benefits and the wonders of the world. If the reasons or purposes one makes the pilgrimage for vary in shape and form, many do not start as spiritual undertakings. Certainly the love for nature, scenic ambiance up close, the love for walking or just freedom from the rat race, most are justifications for pilgrimage seeking. But in the end one catches *Camino* fever.

The differences between the *Camino Portugués* and *Camino Francés* are inherently obvious. For instance, with the exception of the length (240km versus 780km) and time (one taking ten days, the other anywhere from thirty to forty days), all the elements are present. Both *Camino*s were used in the years and centuries past with the same purpose of reaching Santiago de Compostela and of paying homage to the great Apostle, St. James. The *Camino Portugués*, with its start in Porto, is gaining some traction. With the opening of four more hostels on the route during the last ten years and with way marks credibly visible, it offers the modern, younger pilgrim with less time and limited financial resources a challenging alternate route. It does.

Other notable and obvious distinctions also center on the number of pilgrims doing the walk and the romantic, mystical aspects of the *Camino* itself. While the *Camino Portugués* travels through portions of the old Roman road – Via Romana XIX – a road of over two thousand years old, the number of other pilgrims is fewer and the charm less obvious. The scenery on the route is still spectacular; and if one wants more solitude, this *Camino* is the ticket.

Because of the size of the crowds, most villages on the *Camino Francés* came to exist because of the *Camino*. As people from the north of Europe came south, descending on the *Camino*, places to stay and eat also became a natural need. Small communities supporting the needs of the pilgrims evolved. Unless you are a Shirley MacLaine or Paulo Coelho, monasteries of the old ways are no longer a viable solution. Locals with more modern demands in their lives no longer can be counted on as a source of support, considering the quantity of pilgrims passing by. So the itinerary itself creates the atmosphere that renders the *Camino Francés* as a becoming and sought after journey. The connecting dots of small villages and bigger cities abound and thus we witness a nice and dependable structured journeying tradition supporting a modern movement. Naturally, after having *Camino Portugués* under our belt, it was easy to pick the *Camino Francés* as the route of choice.

*In most hostels shoes are not allowed
in the dormitories; naturally..*

11

The First Five, and Only, Stages with Viegas

In prosperity our friends know us,
In adversity we know our friends

Churton Colliss, Aphorisms

The choosing of the *Camino Francés* did not require a long deliberation. The rationale was laid out with an additional appeal, nicely concealed. Viegas became enamored of the idea the minute I disclosed it to him.

A small detail, perhaps with limited value to the long-term or experienced pilgrim, relates to the *Compostela*. The Compostela, a certificate of *Camino* completion, is awarded to any pilgrim that completes a minimum of 100 kilometers on foot or 200 kilometers by bike, during the last stages up to Santiago. Yes, bikers also constitute a measurable group of participants. For Viegas and me, this was a cinch. We got a Compostela in 2008 and Leon, the starting point for our pilgrimage of 2011, would deliver more days and more kilometers. Only age, fatigue and physical aptitude could be an issue.

Leon to Santiago (340kms) represents about forty percent of the typical *Camino Francés*. Our age and lack of time did not allow for the undertaking of the whole enchilada. Too bad. However, starting in Leon had a nice ring to it. Historical, cosmopolitan and friendly are attributes that describe Leon. We learned later, with the "100 kilometer" criteria for the *Compostela* in mind, that many other folks with much more restricted amounts of time would start at stages and points further beyond Leon. And the gaining of one day on the train trip had presented us with a nice challenge - perhaps venturing onto something bolder, a longer trip like walking beyond Santiago, on to the mystique of Finisterre, the end of the land, as it was thought to be one thousand years ago. Bad luck would prove this wish or plan to be unattainable. Bad luck indeed.

On the first morning of the beginning of our journey, the waves of pilgrims were hitting the road and one could already observe the difference in the two *Caminos*. Leaving a hostel in the *Camino Portugués* is a non-event. No crowds and just very few pilgrims. On the *Francés* the waves of pilgrims move within the first two hours and then thin out as the more adroit, fit, younger distance themselves from the lame ducks like ourselves. The former are hares, a description that Viegas very ably coined, whereas we were more like tortoises. Of course tortoises always reach their destination, and we did. Viegas would further describe, on the third day, when the foot problems surfaced, that even crippled or handicapped walkers, if any, passed us by. Indeed we would be the ones that would get most of the ritual greetings of *"Bueno Camino,"* (Good journey). This greeting is typical and reflects a gesture of good wishes and solidarity. It is expressed as we are passed by other pilgrims leaving the hostels for the beginning of the days' journey.

Our destination for the day was Vilar de Mazarife. The 24km journey was nice but presented a test of sorts. It reminded both of us that we were rusty. The village is small and had no municipal hostel. Two private inns were good enough. The second day of the journey was the same picture, of big crowds repeating the act of the day before or days before. As our resistance became less of a factor, the itinerary grew to over 30kms. Astorga was the arrival point. Astorga is a nice city with all the elements of a burgeoning community. Besides a municipal hostel, two private ones were also available. The difference between a municipal and a private hostel depends on the price. Normally the municipal costs a third of a private one. The private hostels also have few beds in total and some even have rooms for two or three.

Leaving Astorga to Rabanal del Camino was not that much of a challenge because the itinerary was shorter – a little over 22kms. Yet the climb was visible and I suspected that Viegas would not keep pace when extending the walk beyond Rabanal. He wanted to but I feared that his feet, like in 2008, would give him trouble. Yet we did venture a few more kilometers; we passed Rabanal and stayed eight kilometers ahead at Foncebadon. This was a bad idea, for the destination did not provide good hostels and Viegas's left foot was acting up badly. Huge blisters from large water bubbles, now broken and dried on their own, were becoming too troublesome to take care of. The enormous medicine cabinet that he had somehow stuffed into his backpack and brought along with him was not of much value. He did not complain. Viegas was determined to move on and convinced himself things would get better.

Although we had gained some good kilometers, Viegas's walking pace was slowing the process. Reaching Ponferrada was an ordeal and a laborious experience. Stops became more frequent and our arrival at Ponferrada was relatively late, diminishing our chances of getting good bunk beds. Good bunk beds are better located in the barracks or on the bottom side as opposed to the upper side. The upper bunk would inevitably create climbing difficulties with a less than good foot. We were unable to get out for a bite of sorts, the difficulties mounted, and the pressure to find viable solutions became more pronounced. Besides, in the face of physical pain and discomfort, I registered that his heroic behavior was taking a toll on his psychological strength. The whole situation was making him more miserable than he should be. He suffered with and by himself and was hiding from me the pain and the difficulty of walking. He had to make adjustments to his walking, like a balancing act, relying more on one foot to avoid the placement of the other on the pavement. The frequent stops also allowed us to analyze the situation as well as to think about alternate courses of action. I inferred that he wanted no part of solutions; his denial was playing a role, one that would fly in the face of what we both had at hand.

The (modified) stage from Ponferrada to Vila Franca del Bierzo, even taking the gain of about eight kilometers, became the reckoning point. More of the same pain and difficulties afflicted him. At the hostel, after consulting with the *hospitalero,* it was determined that he had to see a doctor to cure his foot, and potentially, to accept aborting the trip altogether. *Hospitaleros* are volunteers with pilgrimage experience, with perhaps several pilgrimages on their resume, and they are trained in managing the municipal hostels for a period of time. On average their commitments last two to three weeks. By encouraging me, or more so ordering me, to do the right thing, the hospitalero recognized my dilemma, that I was avoiding sharing the bad news with Viegas. It was not a nice picture. I was torn, but determined.

At the clinic, the doctor was almost flabbergasted as she evaluated what she saw as being an ordeal more appropriate to the medieval ages. Her clinical assessment was candid and it would have been brutal if the evaluation had been pronounced by a male doctor. Females still manifest more tender hearts and they understand males' personal pride well. After cleaning, fixing and dressing the foot, the doctor's final word was for Viegas not to walk another meter, to allow the foot to rest and be restored to a healthy status. Floored and desolated with the outcome, the rest of the night must have not been kind to him. It had not been to me. With the decision ordained for us, the plan was to take him back to Ponferrada by bus and from there proceed with a train trip to Vigo and eventually to southern Portugal. Getting up as early as the other pilgrims, our direction was to the bus station in Vila Franca del Bierzo. We were walking backwards; it was not funny. Waiting at the bus station, we still had time for our café latte and pastry at a nearby café. I concluded at that moment, as he looked at the clock, that he did not want to miss the bus; his mind was well made to get back home soon. The bus trip was somber and reflective. The bigger wounds were not on his feet. They were on his heart and soul and the silent, invisible values he espoused. The feared but not foreseen was happening in front of us.

Many hours later I saw him to the train, hugged and waved him good bye. The trip would not be the same from this point forward. The healing of his feet would take a few weeks but the healing from the outcome would take much longer. Perhaps the scars would stay for good, unless the cure in the form of another pilgrimage would come to be. I was hoping it would happen. Old men don't cry. We did not, but felt like doing so.

Viegas resting with other pilgrims.

John with the hospitalero at Ponferrada Municipal hostel.

Viegas going back home. John taking him to the bus station for
the train ride to Vigo and then to Algarve. A sad morning.

12

Life Goes On - I Continue the Pilgrimage

Courage is almost a contradiction in terms.
It means a strong desire to live taking the forms of readiness to die.

G. K. Chesterton

The train came and left on its destination westbound to Vigo, Spain. Amongst many passengers, certainly some with a Santiago destination, there was Viegas and an enormous assortment of emotions.

We had never discussed the possibility of aborting the pilgrimage of both, in the event one of us had any type of complications, whether on the road or back home. We contemplated adjustments of some kind, like taking an extra day on the whole journey; reducing a day's walk, or other minor changes. The foot problem was not life threatening so the return home for Viegas was not complicated: find appropriate transportation and go easy on the foot. After all, Simas, another of the old acquaintances who lives in Viana do Castelo, the northern part of Portugal, upon learning of our predicament, had volunteered to pick up Viegas at Vigo and assist him back to Algarve, in southern Portugal. This had the look of a doable logistic undertaking, and it was a testimony of the ever-true "what are friends for?" claim. This arrangement, in part, would deflect the emotional blow to Viegas's psyche and soul.

I returned from Ponferrada to Vila Franca del Bierzo by bus, perhaps the same bus we had taken in the morning; just with a different driver. The trip took less than an hour and it was about 12:00 noon when the bus dropped me in the heart of the city. The time in the bus triggered many thoughts and feelings of ambiguity about the rest of the pilgrimage. Definitely, one thought was to continue. But should I stay the rest of the day in Vila Franca del Bierzo, to allow the day's and previous days' events to make some sense and regain some serenity? Or resume the walk right after I arrived at VF del Bierzo, and thus find another life that would keep my eyes occupied, my mind redirected and facing new challenges to be managed? What I needed was to review my _Camino_ guide, refresh my knowledge of the itinerary and decide where to stay for the night. The darn guide was in the backpack away from my reach, i.e., in the bus' luggage compartment. At the bus stop a café was close by and a cold beer was ordered. I did not order any food, fearing unintended and unneeded delays. Just a few minutes would do; to gulp the beer and review my _Camino_ guide. Fortunately, the details in the guide presented this stage as offering nice opportunities such as more than one way – the practical path, the more peaceful and mythical and another short one connecting with both. With about 60% of the "walking" day already gone, the shorter path had the necessary appeal of fewer kilometers and four hostels ahead of me. I thought this was funny, a gift of a choice. Now, with my only familiar and cozy companion well tucked on my back, two pieces of dry meat (beef jerky), a nutrition bar and enough water, resuming the walk only required my legs to oblige and my will to find some traction. As I was leaving town I bumped into another familiar face, of course another road walker. This was an unequivocal validation of the reality that problems occur on the journey; not only to Viegas or me. It was a Japanese pilgrim who had slept in the same hostel just two nights before. Actually Viegas and I slept on the upper bunk beds over his and his wife's. He must have remembered us well for Viegas' and my snores must have been on the heavy side on that night. He proceeded to tell me that his wife was very tired, they would stay in town in a hotel for the day and resume walking on the following day or later. Great idea; perhaps, in retrospect, Viegas and I should have done the same two stages earlier. After all we had some time to spare in our schedule. Too late; now. Ironically, I met the Japanese couple again on my third day after arriving in Santiago. The three day gap between my arrival and theirs made no difference.

Taking the shorter alternate route would make up for time lost. Not a swell decision but one that would restore my sense of comfort about keeping all the stages within the targeted plan. My state of mind was not pleasant or serene; in fact I was a little mad and annoyed. The thoughts of that whole afternoon were occupied with the events of the previous days. Yet my determination gained more strength and desire to carry on with my mission alone, with a defined purpose besides the original intent.

It is not unusual to see pilgrims do the walk alone. If pairs of pilgrims or even larger groups abound on the trails, solo walkers (or loners as I call them) also have their chances. These would carry on their mission alone or would connect with other loners along the way for the moment or for the rest of the journey. The fiction movie *The Way* portraying Martin Sheen, now in theatres, does reveal this aspect of loners.

The plot, in the film, presents four different loners eventually striking up conversations along the route, sharing meals at stops and ending up impacting each other and the collective group. It is a good Hollywood movie, giving a sample of the *Camino* experience, but a movie nevertheless. Some good shots of photography, some little plots, great performances, but at the end of the day it was a project of suave fiction.

The climb towards O'Cebreiro, the previously designated stop, was not bad. Knowing that the climb would be the second steepest – 1,300 meters – of all the stages, my apprehension was real. Of course I would not be able to reach it at the end of the day, unless I would arrive past the hostel time. One of the four hostels, at Valcare, was more than good enough. From that point on to O'Cebreiro the distance was about 16 kilometers. Add another five kilometers to adjust for the steep climb and one faces a stage of over 20 kilometers. On the following day, getting up really early rewarded me; I reached the summit at a very decent time, which encouraged me to forge ahead even further, beyond my plan. As I stopped two hours later, I had gained most of the time lost. It was a feeling of personal victory. My human qualities and defects were in full display here.

Getting up early, as is done by a few early birds, does help to make for good walking in the early stages of the day – with temperatures on the cold side, the stamina is restored - and also to adjust the pace, like slowing it down when fatigue knocks at the door, or during the steep climb on totally uneven trails. Hostels maintain various timetables but on average the latest bed time is 10:00pm and the earliest getting up is 6:00am. In fact, the hospitalero's duties are to house or fill the beds in an orderly manner but also to turn the lights off at 10:00pm. In some instances the hospitalero does not sleep in the hostel. Yet, the rules are widely obeyed, enforced by the fact that no lights are to be on beyond 10:00pm or ordinary noise be made before 6:00am.

As an important note, on earlier stages I had noticed that a small number of pilgrims would get up before 6:00am, politely use their tiny flash lights only around their area, and find the way out with their belongings in tow. I guess I became a good student, for I followed this habit every morning onward. I even took it a step further by having my backpack in ready mode on the night before, with the boots outside as normally recommended for the obvious reason, and then I would change the few clothes from the night for the ones for the day in the bathroom. To be on the road before 6:00am helped considerably. Indeed it is a little discomforting to get up at the typical allotted time, and together with another forty, fifty or sixty folks all trying to use the facilities for eight to ten people at the same time. It is not like rushing out of a football stadium after a sold-out game and bumping each other to get out of the parking lot. But one gets the idea. I became an early bird - a nice and considerate early bird - for sure.

At albergue Mont del Gozo – a bowl of soup with other pilgrims.

Bicyclists also do pilgrimage. John with three from Portugal.

John at a private hostel. Waiting for a very delicious home cooked meal.

At the same private hostel. Beds and dormitories are superior.

13

Inching Closer to Santiago

Everything comes to him who hustles while he waits

Thomas Edison

I had pushed myself, not to the limits but beyond what perhaps I should have done. The thirty plus kilometers were plenty to do on a day that included the climb of O'Cebreiro. Yet my energy was very apparent; my mood was like that of a man seeking quiet revenge for past deeds or misdeeds. This walk put me right on target for the original planned stages. If I continued with the same fervor, I would for sure reach Santiago way before the original targeted arrival. Why and how this new-found energy? I don't know and did not question myself then. But I knew better, that difficulties would come my way and any gains would be given back in some fashion, or worse fashion.

I had six to seven more stages until Santiago. The way marks were already revealing the kilometers needed to reach my destination. Triacastela, Sarria, Portomarin, Palas de Rei, Arzua, Arca do Pino, Monte do Gozo, would be stopping stages. All of these good size towns or communities offered various degrees of challenges as well as rewards. Triacastela, after passing O'Cebreiro, was the longest of the walks. In appropriate fashion the penalty was to arrive late, beyond 5:00pm. All the three hostels (municipal and private) were full and now the fear - that I would have to knock at doors and beg for shelter, home or barn, - hit home. However, a private room was found, and that night, it was just me alone, with a good hall bathroom for three, no noise, no snoring. This in itself was a benefit of multiple dimensions: rest your tired legs and feet from the long (the longest) days' walk, solitude for the heart and the soul, and then free to hit the road on the following day with an "early bird's" gusto. All the other hostels on the rest of the way were reached in ample time and with the first-come, first-served results well attained. Experience and good planning were operating magnificently.

As I shared in another chapter, it would not do my story justice to detail all of the events, experiences, and encounters; the touches and the feelings accumulated and relayed, here in this writing project. Each of the remaining stages brought on or presented their own challenges and degrees of quiet excitement. Many of the faces, those we had encountered in the early stages, would appear again. Even two or three people inquired about Viegas. These are stories for another time.

There was nothing transformative on the Way. For sure, if I thought at times that life would never be the same, I was also sure that I left much behind, ignored. The beauty of the whole experience was the expectation that the *Camino* fever would never desert me. The fever is felt, is transmitted by the smallest of all things, and the recognition that something somehow from above was having an invisible, subtle but real impact on you. In our own world one is impacted by everything that surrounds us: people, the schedules, the projects, the responsibilities, whether real or invented. We rush to get the platter full and in the process trigger our own powerlessness and stress. On the other hand, if it is not full we feel miserable and again stressed. Yah, we've got to fill this thing, this platter, again. A small platter would be good enough, if we just tamed the anxiety. The *Camino*, in its simplest moments, or some other wholesome, worthwhile escapade with good doses of solitude, helps you to dig inside and causes revelations of pure beauty and refreshing clarity.

It does not take long, with the simplicity of the journey, to adjust to living or passing the days with rudimentary means: simple meals, sharing a room with twenty or forty or sixty other human beings who, believe it or not, look exactly like you. Whatever things you left behind in our world of typical comfort, even if just for a few days or weeks, became no longer important to you. How funny it is that we can now – on the *Camino* – say with absolute certainty that what we considered real needs were just exercises of wishes. The value of things in the past perhaps were not that big. Just inventions of the moment, or the kind of environment we choose to be in. Then, it is not difficult to realize and comprehend the finite nature of things. Yes, there is an end for and to everything. There is also a very real recognition that all of us carry a lot of trash – possessions, feelings, emotions, prejudices – along our life's journey. Getting rid of some of the baggage could alleviate the weight of the journey. Really!

The daily telephone call from Donalda came between 4:00 and 5:00pm. The calls were brief, more like an alarm clock reminding me that I left my wife, my lover, the mother of my kids behind. The calls were about how I was doing or she was doing. No summaries on what was happening in the world, such as the stock market crashing or the birth of another war. Even when Donalda notified me of the death of the mother of a friend of ours, it was preceded by an apology for sharing it. She was doing well, finding her way around, clinging to some activities and friends at the local church in Lagoa and hoping the days would go fast. I was proud for her resourcefulness and taking charge of things. While there, it is normal for her to lean on me for some of the basic stuff. "No, I do not want to drive; you do it," were her normal responses when confronted with choices. "After all these streets are narrow. I need to avoid trouble." The narrow streets were real, and excuses as well.

The phone calls after Viegas's episode became more inquisitive as to the status of my emotions or about the difficulty of walking alone. To all questions of the kind my answers were nothing but positive. Not that I did not miss Viegas, but the solo experience was equally good, with some thrills along the way. Calls from Sá and Baltazar, another friend in Portugal, came almost daily. The calls were short in duration for all the applicable reasons, especially the cost of cell phone calling. These, if unchecked, can add up your pilgrimage bill. All these calls had the same purpose – how I was doing? Their encouragement was also evident and in some way refreshing for my little ego. Viegas also called twice, the first time a few days after his arrival back home. He was curious where I was, relative to the stages attained. I wanted to be discreet but somehow he recognized I was making very good time. He said, "now with the pain in the butt out of the way, you are traveling like a hare." I replied that I was more like an agile turtle with a thin and less heavy shell – my backpack. The other time was after I had reached Santiago. I could not see his tears, but interpreted that they were there. He wanted that experience to be his, too. So did I. He was happy for me.

Our own (original) planned schedule indicated that we would arrive at Santiago on a Friday and Donalda would take a flight from San Miguel to Lisbon, would stay with our friends Sá and his wife Angelina for a night, then proceed up north of Portugal to connect with Simas and his wife Teresa, and then the final rendezvous with me in Santiago. Actually, with the good management of the remaining stages, Santiago appeared within my reach on Wednesday. Instead of advancing, I opted to stay at Monte Gozo or Monte del Gozo, at an enormous hostel – actually two compounds of almost army barracks that could house anywhere from 600 to 800 people. I did not need that much; just a bed and a bathroom not far from my bunk bed. In reality I had a room with beds to accommodate twenty. Two other pilgrims arrived later and became my roommates for the night. Interestingly enough, one of them, whom I alluded to earlier, represented pilgrims that are perpetual walkers. This one told me he had logged fourteen thousand kilometers in about twenty-two months. He was, must still be, Swiss, and had walked most of the twelve *Caminos*. He showed me six credentials, revealing at least five hundred locations he had stopped at. The man, a thin, hippie looking type with a small beard and semi-long hair, was gracious in his manners and attention. The callous on his feet proved to me he was a walking machine. I could not tell his age, and I did not ask either, but he looked not to be beyond forty years old.

Monte Gozo is just about five kilometers from Santiago. This choice allowed me to arrive at Santiago on the following day, in no hurry and more aware of my surroundings. This hostel is enormous but rarely filled to capacity unless extraordinary events take place, like the visit of Pope John Paul in the mid 1990's. It is correct to note that this place was of vast importance to pilgrims of the distant past. Once pilgrims would arrive at this mountain, they could already see, far away, the towers and the steeples of the cathedral. *Gozo* (meaning Joy or Mountain of Joy) was the rewarding feeling that Santiago was within close reach.

Another reason for my stay in Monte Gozo was influenced by my knees. At least one of them was acting funny and very soon, about a kilometer or two in distance, I started limping and walking with noticeable difficulty. I took it as a message from above that unnecessary heroism did not count and deserved no medals. With difficulty I moved around the compound, washed all my clothes, and then let the sun, still vibrant, do the drying. A good and generous plate of warm soup cooked and served by a Polish *hospitalero* and enjoyed by a couple other dozen pilgrims complimented a quasi finish of the Pilgrimage. The night was equally peaceful. I guess I deserved it.

14

Arriving At and Staying In Santiago

An atheist is a man who has no invisible means of support.

Bishop Fulton Sheen

I did not follow my plan of the night before to the letter. Instead I took my time to leave the hostel. There was nothing there to keep me entertained either; no game room, no bar, no TV, no Internet nor companions to chat with or exchange observations. But rushing anything was not necessary either. I had two pieces of fruit and some water, and that would be sufficient for me to get going until I would run into a bakery or a coffee shop for my pastry, *tostada* (bread and butter with jelly) and latte. Empty moments always invite deep thinking, some debriefing on everything that has accumulated in your brain. Many thoughts populated my mind but always one survived the ordeal: the pilgrimage was reaching its destination and new chapters would be around the corner.

With plenty of rest my legs felt fine; my knee did not ache, so I was ready for the road. In 2008, entering Santiago, Viegas and I had a heck of a time following the marks towards the cathedral and had to ask questions here and there. This time I paid attention to the streets and learned that once you enter the new and more modern Santiago, the marks are found only on the sidewalks of the streets leading to the Cathedral. Beautiful bronze shells, of about three-four inches in diameter and mimicking the real sea shells, are implanted into the sidewalk every one to two hundred meters, through the streets, (more like alleys) veering here or there. If you get distracted or lost and find no marks, the sure way is to walk back until you locate the reliable direction. Or, you can ask for directions. Large yellow arrows are normally seen on trails, in small villages and byways. About 200 kilometers from

Santiago, the trails, old roads or intersections, in addition to the yellow arrows, are well marked with standalone way marks dressed with the traditional symbol of the sea shell and the kilometer distance to Santiago.

By 10:00am I was entering Santiago, with soft emotions surging, but nothing else. I am not saying that this wasn't a big deal, but the novelty had waned a bit. The entrance route from *Camino Francês* is different from the *Camino Português*. The *Português* meanders a little longer on the modern Santiago. Otherwise, nothing dramatic to note.

I was surprised, as one enters the Plaza (*Praza do Obrodoiro*) to the Cathedral, to see an ocean of little tents of all colors dotting a great portion of the ample plaza space; perhaps half the space of the square. They appeared organized, all on one side as if something of great importance was about to take the stage. There were many signs and little banners, not with messages of "repent" or something like that, but reflecting the condition of the times. No, it was not the "Occupy Wall Street" movement extending its reach to Santiago. Yet, it had, I learned later, some similar overtones.

At 10:00 am many pilgrims were already strolling within the perimeter of the plaza. Some could have been arrivals of the day before or others who had shorter routes to reach Santiago. It was only at about 11:00 am that the swelling became visible and I recognized many faces I had encountered on the early stages of my own journey. I must have done well. With an early arrival, I made my way inside the cathedral for the 12:00 noon Mass. Now, free of the backpack, which I left in a storage place around the cathedral, actually at the *Oficina del Peregrino* (pilgrims office), I found myself a place to sit. Soon the cathedral would fill to its capacity, standing room only, with pilgrims as well as many tourists.

Besides Masses celebrated in other churches around the Cathedral, there is one official Mass dedicated to the pilgrims every day. My Spanish is not that good but the message sounded typically the same: praise and respect for the pilgrim, the journey and everything it portends to mean and impart. Normally it is celebrated with a dozen priests and/ or a bishop. The pomp is tamed but real. This day, because it does not happen every day, one of the rituals included the ritual of the *Botafumeiro*. A giant, I mean *giant*, incense burner hung from the ceiling and centered on the large altar area, swinging left and right with the help of, I guess another dozen priests, *Tiraboleiros*. Yes, it requires that many hands to move this incense burner. The original purpose, a few centuries past, I am told, was to fumigate the sweaty or perhaps dirty pilgrims.

Another symbolic detail or step during the Mass, and one that the priests truly enjoyed executing, was mentioning the pilgrims who had completed the journey and thus were rewarded with the *Compostela*. No names were mentioned but a recitation of the number of pilgrims from each country: *thirty-eight from Spain, fourteen from Germany, eleven from United States, eighteen from France, and so on.* I knew that the US tally did not include me; I had only registered and obtained my *Compostela* after the Mass. Of course I would count on the following day.

At the end of Mass there were hugs, tender moments and tear-eyed faces from many a pilgrim to another. I did enter the hugging with two people that I remembered well from the *Camino*. One even recalled that I had a companion and inquired about his absence.

With plenty of time for the rest of the afternoon and more than two days to spare before Donalda's arrival, the solitude was not that much welcome. Writing or taking some other notes of things, of the environment, the people's joy, did not inspire me either. Galicia's weather was balmy at this time of the year. Soaking on the warm afternoon and around the sidewalk cafes and restaurants I became a tourist - a solo tourist.

A pint of beer and some tapas helped the moment take its own meaning. There were people everywhere; whether locals or tourists, these were indistinguishable. But not the pilgrims; perhaps with cleaner clothes, and with no need to be fumigated, yet they could stand out and be recognized with ease. In fact, theirs were the faces of happier people. The others had more serious business, as if their lives lacked wholesome fulfillment. My solitude no longer mattered. Gazing at the whole scene, replete with action and joy transmitted by the pilgrims, made me feel happy.

I have a weakness but one that does put me to shame. For some reason, we (my wife and I) rarely arrive at an airport with plenty of time to spare. In a "rushing" mode I am not aware of my environment; I just wait for my group number (normally the last one) to be called and search the whole plane for carry-on luggage space. However, on stopovers, long waits in the airports do not bother me. I enjoy admiring the

whole ambiance created by the movement of streams of people coming from or going to somewhere: some rushing like maniacs or chick-
ens with their heads cut off, others reading their second book, or others
totally concentrated on their laptop computers, and in the very, very
present time, others wrapped up in other more modern equipment
such as iPods, iPhones, iPads, "I" this or "I" that. Even when some
passengers, frustrated for a variety of reasons, put into play their loud
arguing skills with the airline personnel at the gate counters, they draw
my attention and trigger various reactions. Mostly I feel sorry for airline folks and feel disdain for the bone-headed complainers. For me,
this is fascinating, a fascinating show. I don't even mind being bumped
anymore. A voucher would come in handy, plus another two hours of
free entertainment.

After getting my *Compostela* – the certificate of completion - I walked
a couple of kilometers to one of the two large municipal hostels for the
night, and the next two. This one is large, previously the quarters of a
Seminary, with housing for over four hundred people on three floors.
There are rooms with many beds, that is where the similarity with the
other hostels ends. There are no bunk-beds; disposable bed sheets are
available, as well as pillows. Bathrooms are plenty, well structured and
with more privacy. The eating area is large, with a kitchen equipped
nicely with useful appliances. Having a private locker helps, and for
me, as I needed to camp here for at least three nights, it was just right.

The next days – Friday and Saturday – would be free days. Of course,
Finisterre was on our radar at the very start of the journey. If everything had gone well, including our physical and emotional condition,
we thought we would have three days to spare for an additional walk
(100klms) to Finisterre. That didn't happen. Still, I wanted to see Finisterre. A two-hour bus ride to Finisterre took care of business. It driz-
zled, and then it really rained, so that came to be part of the trip and
the stay at Finisterre. My idea was not unique, for many familiar faces
filled a couple buses. I can't fathom if their ordeals or ideas were like
mine; it was nice to be in known company.

For someone who was born and lived on an island for over two
decades, finding the ocean always generates great emotions, warm feelings. Even when the most menacing, potent waves, with rushing white
sheets of water find and hit their match, the rocks, and spew showers
and water foam on all directions. Observing this is a warm feeling for
me; it is nostalgic.

Saturday, another free day, was used to see Santiago – in and around – up close. I did not measure the kilometers I walked; it was not important for this type of long day walk, similar to walks in other big cities like Rome, Paris, London or Madrid. Without a backpack I was a tourist, a tourist on economic transportation – feet and legs. With the day fast reaching its conclusion, I was really anxious for Sunday to come.

When Sunday came, with my breakfast routine duly and gladly observed, I returned to the hostel to fetch my faithful companion, my backpack, or (rucksack as the British often say). My legs, as if they were GPS trained, directed me towards the cathedral and the Praza do Obrodoiro. More and more pilgrims were filling the square, and this being Sunday, they would be joined by tourists – foreign or Spaniards – familiar with these shortcut pilgrimages, or visits. The numbers were much higher than at the Thursday Mass, naturally. A large group of students from the University of Michigan was happily taking pictures of scenes worthy of snapshots. I asked to take a picture of them; the bright colors of the University banner and their very happy demeanors would reveal credible proof of a worthwhile experience.

Donalda and her entourage of Sá and Angelina, Simas and Teresa connected with me at the Plaza. I was thrilled to see Donalda and the entourage as well. Donalda was impressed with the cathedral and interested in everything to know and see about the Apostle. Yet her thrill at the arriving, in the face of the much talked about *Camino* and the undertaking, was mild and contained. It could not have the same impact on her as it had on me in 2008, and to a different extent in 2011. I did the walk. She did not.

I occasionally revisit a universally and often expressed truth: *it is not the destination that matters or is important; it is the journey.* I agree, and she accepted it.

Typical scene of pilgrims arriving and relaxing at Santiago.

*College students also do pilgrimages. University of Michigan
is proudly displayed at Plaza do Obrodoiro, Santiago.*

Credentials from a "walking machine." A pilgrim who housed with John at Mt. Gozo logged over 15,000 kilometers in about two years, consecutively.

15

Enjoying Our Friends' Company

Forsake not an old friend; for the new is not comparable to him:
A new friend is as new wine; when it is old,
thou shalt drink it with pleasure

Bible – Ecclesiasticus 9-10

After we all had a very Spanish, or more likely Galician, late lunch in Santiago, we made our return trip in Simas's van towards Portugal. By the way, Spain still has distinct regions. Besides the Basque, Galicia is equally proud, although not necessarily as vociferous, about their heritage and place in history. In fact Galicia was in the 11th century a continuation of Portugal. Their dialect, a language in itself, is very close to the Portuguese language. Politics of the times – the 11th century - caused rifts to erupt and Galicia became part of the Spanish kingdoms. Sometimes I think the whole peninsula – Iberia – should be a federation of the two countries. They have their own identities but a common role as Iberians.

It took a little less than two hours to cross the border and half an hour to reach Simas's home in Viana do Castelo. Viana, as most Portuguese refer to it, is very pretty. Encroached on the west side by the sea and on the east side by the mountains, it sprawls nicely and graciously.

Together with Sá and his wife, we stayed at Simas's for a little over two days. As beneficiaries of Teresa's excellent culinary skills, the two days did not last long. Teresa not only cooks brilliantly, but she enjoys doing so for friends and family. When I come across good home cooking, my first reaction is to compliment the chef for putting a lot of love in it. She is good.

Rewinding the clock to old times, it does not take long for the memory to flash back to comfortable and fun moments. We have been able to visit them every three years, at least, during the last twelve years. Even if the Azores and continental Portugal are separated by about one thousand miles, or a two-hour plane ride, these are small obstacles as we find ways to connect. We reminisced about old times and concluded that these visits represent the fertilizer that keeps the friendship very much alive.

The four of us – Sá, Viegas, Simas and I – were born in, or are at least from, different regions in Portugal. Simas is from up north, Sá in the center, from the suburbs of Lisbon, Viegas from the deep south, in the Algarve. I am from further away in the Atlantic Ocean. That is the Azores, those nine little dots that Google Earth barely recognizes unless you zoom in. They are gorgeous islands, remnants of volcanic eruptions perhaps millions of years ago. They are volcanic paradises.

Our friendship started a little over forty-eight years ago, when we became members of a battalion preparing to serve in a guerrilla war in Angola, Africa, then a colony of Portugal. The Portuguese actually claimed it to be an overseas province. The rebels dreamed of an environment of pure emancipation and liberation of their regions from the colonial power of other European nations - British, French, Italians, Spanish, Dutch and so on. Indeed, World War II not only settled the military power game, but also indirectly or directly put into motion liberation movements throughout the world of nations dominated by the European powers. Starting in the Middle East, the Far East and extending into the African Continent, the domino effect was on its way to becoming a reality. The French were suffering defeats in prolonged wars in Indochina and Algeria. The British astutely formed agreements of mutual cooperation, and with the others offering little resistance, they got the emancipation job done. Only the Portuguese, after being unceremoniously kicked out of small territories in India in 1960, stubbornly resisted the liberation movements of the colonies of Angola, Mozambique and Guinea-Bissau. Granted, these liberators were not entirely genuine. Most of the fomenters were primarily instigated and financed by foreign communist regimes. It was a war on three fronts that lasted from the early sixties until 1974, when Portugal freed itself from a long dictatorship. This was a war that drained Portuguese finances, divided the country and offered no consolation prizes.

The battalion was formed in August 1963, and in January 1964 Angola became our professional arena and home. Simas, Viegas and

I were platoon sergeants and Sá assigned as the Company's fleet and fleet maintenance Sergeant. We were together for almost three years, day in and day out in each other's faces, so the stage was set for a strong bond and friendship to emerge and constitute an organism in itself. None of us were saints, but we found ways to co-exist nicely. We had to, for there was nowhere to go and have fun. Of course, our enormous amount of time there - the experiences, close calls and the like – are enough material; stories of real interest to many and to us in particular. Thus our occasional times together always serve as the stage for memory lane revisits.

Once our assignments were over, in early June 1966, and we returned to Portugal, young lads like us were ready to face the ordinary world, start our professional careers, get married and form families. I married a month upon my return and soon after I embarked on my own odyssey in America. That was in October 1966. I remember it so well.

On those two days in Viana, the three of us discussed at length the episodes of the Camino pilgrimage and in much detail the bad luck with our friend Viegas. Before we had considered the possibility, but not committed to, the three couples going to meet with Viegas, down south in the Algarve, after the pilgrimage ended. His emotional and psychological let-down had been duly discussed by us, we had unveiled some scenarios towards doing the right thing. A couple of telephone calls revealed that the time was right to follow up on the original possibility, and to spend a few days with him and his wife Maria do Carmo. We were relieved, as we were certain that our plan would serve multiple purposes.

Donalda and I rode with Sá, southbound towards his home. We spent a couple more days there, until Simas joined us for our third and last stage of our friendship reunion. Viegas was ready for us and closure was about to perform its magic.

Algarve by now is a very well known and sought after region for summer vacations. It stretches over one hundred kilometers of beaches, with warm and clear waters, and state-of-the-art resorts, and these vacation spots on the radars of travel agents and Hollywood/ European stars seeking anonymity. The stories that filled the newspaper and television about the kidnapping or disappearance of Madelyn McCann, a British kid, a few years back, were not necessary to put Algarve on the map. The region deserves its vacation accolades. When we are there we rarely go to the beaches; instead we splurge on more close-to-nature endeavors or spend our hours on food, drinking and good conversations.

Viegas's foot got cured, but he was still limping on the other foot. Favoring one over the other caused an over-compensation. His spirits had returned and he showed clear signs that he was almost ready for another journey. He now knows how to better prepare himself properly for undertakings of this magnitude. We walked for a couple of hours, without a backpack, and he regained the necessary confidence. I hope so.

Friends from the army at Viegas's home – (l-r) Sá, John, Simas and Viegas

*With friends from Continental Portugal at Algarve –
food and wine, the glue that connects friendship.*

*At Viegas's home in Algarve. Celebration of a
nice reunion called for champagne.*

16

Ending "Too Much of a Good Thing"

God grant me the serenity to accept things I cannot change
The courage to change the things I can and the wisdom to know the difference

-Anonymous

We were back in São Miguel, happy but exhausted. It was an exhaustion of a different kind - not physical. After all, we were not working in the mines or doing hard labor. We still had eleven days before returning to our home in California.

There were still leftover and undone small projects and work to do on our new bathroom. We also made it a point to reduce the speed of everything we were doing and to relax, just by ourselves. It was also a time to review the year, although it was only at the beginning of the second half. The first half was greater than, way greater than, years past. We asked, My Lord, what are we doing? Do we really have the stamina and physical means for an encore, for more activity programmed for four weeks, starting on the third week of July? The answer, albeit weird, was yes, we do.

Paulo Soares is my godson and the one we have relied on for power-of-attorney representation; first on a small plot of land, now sold, and second on our home, purchased in 2006. We have a close relationship with him, his wife Laura, and their teenage sons, Alexandre and Rafael. We love them and they love us; we are close. At one time I commented on the reality of the relationship and he was quick to reply, "Sometimes friends are greater than family," adding, "we do not choose our brothers and sisters or cousins; we do choose our friends." That's a nice and intelligent answer to a sensitive question, and to reality.

Time and again we had extended an invitation to them to spend time with us in California. The typical answer had seldom changed: "when our finances are in affordable shape, and on the condition that Laura visits her place of birth." Fair enough. The first condition, though we would reduce the money part by hosting them at no cost, was on their shoulders; the second – in some measure their own choice – did transfer weight to my own shoulders.

Kitimat, far north in British Columbia, is not, naturally, next door to the San Francisco Bay Area. Taking a plane trip from the San Francisco Bay Area to Vancouver is not a big deal, quite the contrary, it is routinely done on a well travelled corridor. Vancouver to Kitimat, a small city that is deeply isolated and home to less than fifteen thousand people, is another story. In money terms, the budget for four people is not too bad. Eight people - their entourage and us - is a larger number, demanding an exercise of math, good math. In any case, exercising their choices, they would arrive in California a couple of weeks after our own return home. Were we nuts? Didn't I ask that before? You get the picture.

We arrived home in California, again exhausted but evidently happy. Aren't vacations designed for one to relax and restore one's resistance reservoir for the activities of our own rat race world? The reality is startling: I have yet to come across any friend of mine who has claimed that their vacation was relaxing. And if these friends have kids, like the vacations that our sons take, forget it. It is almost like whispering: "bring my job back; it will be more relaxing, sane and reliable."

Our sons, their wives, and above all, our grand-kids were very happy to see us again. They actually inspected us thoroughly to figure out if the long absence had modified our looks, increased or stalled our aging and above all to see if we were ready for some baby-sitting assignments, or to simply be part of their lives again. The older son has kids with ages ranging from thirteen to ten to five; they do not require baby-sitting; just adult supervision. Our youngest son, with one kid only, requires a two-day a month thing. But our middle son, with seven, five, three year-old girls, is another story. I was told, in secrecy by another brother, that Victor missed us the most. We do not do any scheduled babysitting or adult supervision nowadays. By request, yes, otherwise it would be utterly expensive; we are the "emergency" vehicle. The kicker is that the "emergency" commitment has turned into the go-to for any little or major need. Take or pick up kids from school, a doctor's visit, a luncheon with a friend, night out for the parents, a weekend getaway, etc., etc. and more etc.

Donalda and I did anticipate that at one point in our lives, more in the later years, that our role as grandparents would require us to meet one defined need – to assist all of them with babysitting requests. Our three sons live within reasonable proximity to us. The youngest is an hour away, and then the oldest, half an hour away, and the middle son is almost a strenuous walk away. When you are equipped with a cell phone, the connection – emergency or trivial – is assured. Our "Write what you ask, or need" mandate rarely happens. Not even the warning "one of these days, there will be no babysitting" works or modifies their behavior. They are very busy, I guess.

My other visualization of this is more romantic, or philosophical. See, I am getting better. Really, our grand kids are lucky for having another generation to be part of their lives. We are lucky, too. In the end, being around our grandkids for some conversation and bonding does help them, whether by validating or editing their parent's parenting, culture, and methods. We are busy with them but equally very blessed.

Including our friends Carlos and Beatriz Paes, Paulo and the rest of the gang from San Miguel, Azores, came as planned. Besides my wife and my sons, I had never spent such a long time – four weeks – with the same group of people. By the time they returned home, all of our secrets had been revealed and our habits interchangeably copied. My minivan, with a capacity for eight people, was good enough for trips around California. Kitimat – over sixteen hundred miles away from our home - was another challenge. Only a twelve-seat passenger van could accommodate such long trips. We got it, and what a relief. In fact, the van would eventually accommodate another couple of friends we had planned to visit and stay with while in Vancouver. Aside from his driving – scary, that is - Clovis and Fernanda Amado were great hosts who also served as able guides from Vancouver to Kitimat. They knew the area, and had once lived in Kitimat for a long time.

Kitimat, in northwest British Columbia and two hundred miles east of southern Alaska, is a town, now in decline, that was built in the 1950's exclusively to support aluminum mines and related services. Deep water channels and other characteristics made the region ideal. Canada, around this time, was still in its expansion mode, conquering the west with the building of railways and exploring and developing their natural resources. Expansion requires people, and people are not fabricated so quickly. Immigration became the answer and many Portuguese folks answered the call. Laura's parents were some of those early immigrants. And so it was that Laura came to see light as a Kitimatan, and/or a Canadian. At the age of two, Laura, with her mother and sister, returned to the Azores and San Miguel.

Laura always mentioned one day connecting with her birth place, and it came to be in August, 2011. Strange and long distance wishes were now fulfilled. We shared in her emotional reactions when, with the help of some references, she came to see the home in which she was born. I would have felt the same.

Our trip was marvelous in every respect. It was a magnificent adventure for us, and for them a treasure, for sure. Driving up through Northern California towards the states of Oregon and Washington gave us a great view of the immense dimension of the Pacific territories. The trip from Vancouver to Kitimat, another eight hundred miles away, continued the discovery of land still unspoiled and untamed. A return trip, partially on a fifteen hour, huge ferry boat crossing through the Pacific's Inside Passage culminated a journey of wonders.

What a great year. I am done, I have travelled enough.

Friends from San Miguel – inside a 12 passenger wagon.
(The two front rows, four passengers not shown.)

At Kitimati, British Columbia, Canada. Complete map sign at a park.

Friends from San Miguel with friends from Vancouver at a Vancouver beach – (l-r) Carlos Pais, Donalda and John, Fernanda and Clovis Amado, Alexandre Soares, Beatriz Pais, Laura Silva and Paulo Soares.

17

The Year's Home Stretch

*The salary of the chief executive of a large corporation is not
a market value award for achievement.
It is frequently in the nature of a warm personal gesture
by the individual to himself.*

John Kenneth Galbraith

Donalda is fully retired. She still has some physical and emotional
energy to invest in a professional environment. Current conditions
remind her that it is time to find other venues to channel this energy,
such as arenas of personal and community interest. She has found her
stride and is being rewarded with many moments of joy.

I retired early, at age fifty-nine, at the beginning of 1999. After almost
thirty-four years of a banking career, the time became ripe to hang it
up or switch my garments, the uniform of a retail banker to that of a
drifter. Not really. I had accumulated much valuable experience and
know-how (although it was not utilized in the last years of my professional journey) that would be useful in the years that followed.

We find ourselves on the last stretch of our enormously and fully
lived 2011. For my part, I recognized for some time that my remaining part-time consulting job would come to an end at some point. I
needed to do justice to all concerned – Creative Wood, my family, and
my own needs and aspirations. On the road to seventy-one, I still nour-
ish some aspirations: quiet, tamed, below the radar; even selfish aspirations. Service clubs, social involvement and deeds of charity have been
part of my life since the age of eighteen. I see myself as always engaged
in some form of support group or another. The word "no" is very difficult to pronounce when confronted with requests for service. *Yes*, or
why not, I will find a way, has preempted the impulse to say *"no."* Now

a certain resistance has surfaced, and exploring other (small) worlds, like my own inner world, has piqued my, now undisputed, interest. I am lucky, and very comfortable with confronting all the present challenges.

Including family members who own their own business, I have had three consulting jobs which made great use of my skills and experience. The third one is still going, just as it appears the Duracell battery wants to keep on going. The owners of Creative Wood, besides being good friends, have come to rely on my two-bits of advice and wisdom. However, my prolonged periods of absence have caused a quandary of sorts. So I've reached a painful decision: I will not retire from them; I'll just fade away. Officially I am still in.

These almost twelve years of professional engagement after retiring from Bank of America have been the most fulfilling. I recall that someone once said: *when you love what you do, you will never work a day in your life.* My last ten years have been proof of that belief.

Perhaps I could have had that experience of *"not working a day in my life"* in the years past, but life is what it is. I must confess that my first dozen years, at least, at Bank of America really were that fruitful, fulfilling, and above all, meaningful. New in the country, without college degrees or credentials, Bank of America became my country, my home, my school and my avenue towards professional fulfillment. The Bank was that good. Not the best paying job in town, but a job with all the equipment to make me feel productive, useful, and in the end, a contributor of value.

In the late sixties and all of the seventies, Bank of America continued to sail, like a solid aircraft carrier, navigating with authority and projecting the legacy of A. P. Giannini, the founder and the banking genius of his time, and now the envy of current bankers. What a contrast. The period that Giannini lived was as challenging and chaotic as that of today, but the results are entirely and diametrically different.

The bank and the banker that made history are nothing short of miraculous. This achievement is more dramatic because it lasted very long, it impacted a wide range of people, it caused many and various innovations to take place, but above all it accomplished this despite an environment of jealousy, envy and incompetence in the financial arena. Like the '49ers Bill Walsh's "West Coast Offense", Amadeo Peter Giannini ("AP") invented "retailed banking" – a branch of the whole, a warm presence in every location - as we have now had it for quite some time. His impact on the life of consumers, particularly the ordinary, without-a-bank consumers, was of unparallel importance. He ranked as high as the Fords in the auto industry, Sears/Roebuck in retail or department stores, or the more contemporary game changers such as Hewlett Packard, Bill Gates or Steve Jobs. These and many others left extraordinary legacies. People like these keep our hopes alive. Others just make us cringe with pain.

The dawning of the 20th century could not foretell the many discoveries, improvements, changes, and innovations that made America "great". The power of a few – the drivers of capitalism and the political machine - would eventually be tested against that of genuine dreamers, unselfish and heroic drivers of wealth alone. While the former prevailed for many years, reincarnating and reproducing themselves forever, the latter would come to challenge the status quo.

Banking in A. P. Giannini's era was the same that had prevailed in the eras past – it was only for a few. Not the few and the now much publicized "top one percent", but the privileged of *who you know* and those of means. By founding Bank of America - actually Bank of Italy for many years - in 1904 in San Francisco, AP (as Giannini was popularly known) brought banking to the little fellow, a bank for people who had not used one before. There is nothing in today's banking landscape, or in the last twenty years, that resembles AP's dream or legacy. In the early times, Giannini's salary was $200.00 per month – three times the salary of the average employee. As years progressed, the Bank's fortunes increased, and the banker would see his salary grow as well; but always commensurate with everyone else's performance; it was significantly modest. I knew that.

When I joined Bank of America in late 1966, the world was not in terrible shape. Confusion, ambivalence, and tentativeness were conditions, in my view, reining in many quarters of the globe. World War II was behind us, cold war politics was the fare of the era, the hippie and easy-going love generation were in full swing, and the war in Vietnam was polarizing the nation. The civil rights movement had gained some necessary traction and respect. Yet since I was new to the country, these symptoms and conditions were negligible to me. While many were occupied with the drama of the day, I was just happy and proud to be in America and ready to do my part. The Bank was impressive and, figuratively speaking, transmitted vibes of multiple colors, shapes and scents. Naturally, compared with from where I had come, everything in America impressed me. AP had already passed away. His patented legacy was not recited to us – new employees – on any day of the calendar; there were no salutes or pledges of any kind. But as I progressed in my career I became curious and determined to know more about the man that made history. What I found is worth sharing.

In 1906, during the San Francisco earthquake, just a couple of years barely walking (as a Bank) AP demonstrated the ability, the courage, and the initiative to do the right thing for all, whether clients, would-be clients, or the people of San Francisco. The earthquake caused fires everywhere, buildings were collapsing, people were in panic, and businesses closed; it was traumatic enough to confound anyone. Bank of America's building, next door to a jail – so it was better protected than by a security guard – was not damaged that much. AP, however, feared that some fires could extend to the building. He removed all the cash and gold from the safe, and hid them on the bed of a horse buggy, covered by crates of oranges, and moved to a safer place. With this money and the bank records, AP knew the Bank's position, and got ready for business. It was an outdoor business, offering plenty of encouragement with flea market type advertising. The Bank took charge. The other bankers, typically insulated, were confused; they were no match to AP. $80,000.00 in cash (to cover $800,000.00 of deposits) was not much money even then, but it was seed money, and the incentives were there for more money, for deposits and consequently more lending.

Little ads were created on a moment's notice, circular letters were sent to notify depositors that small withdrawals were allowed and that loans for reconstruction were available. It was enough to instill confidence that the positive was possible. Ordinary people were inspired by the actions of the little Bank of Italy, while the big power banks appeared to be physically and mentally overmatched. Great people move; they become agents of change. Others advertise gun power.

With the earthquake behind him and San Francisco, AP's vision of helping the little guy could only be carried out on a larger scale, by expanding his ideas and dreams beyond San Francisco to other communities in the Bay Area and California. And who knows? Even beyond the state. Branch banking became the target, the driver of the dream. Regulation for the sake of regulation is not good. Regulation to control the excesses or to protect the lambs from the wolves is not only proper, but it is also the guardian of the rewards of functioning capitalism. During the first quarter of the century and a little beyond, AP fought with tooth and nail for the removal of the barriers to branch banking. Eventually the stock market crash of 1930 would prove that the sins were from the money changers, not the honest drivers of the economy's life blood. By the end of the first quarter AP was well known, respected, and feared on both coasts. In some manner the east coast, mainly represented by New York - one of the two money centers of the planet - did not give much support or credence to the west coast experiment. Some disdain was visible. The advances of branch banking reached Los Angeles and every corner of the state. Deposits grew and loans were available for every honest and productive undertaking.

With branch banking a reality, with an ever increasing number of depositors and borrowers, AP's energy and brains turned to the remaking of banking itself, making it more functional as the ideal conduit of wealth for all. During the great depression, similarly inspired by the actions of President Franklin D. Roosevelt, AP supported every business enterprise, whether war related or related to the expansion of the California economy. Factories, shipyards, bridges and agriculture received his attention and support. The building of the Golden Gate Bridge, the iconic landmark visited by thousands and thousands of people from every part of the globe, is appropriately credited to many, including the Engineer Joseph B. Straus and the banker A. P. Giannini. While some frowned at the enormous amount of money needed to finance the project, AP saw it otherwise. Connecting the north to the south counties would only generate more economic growth – it was good enough to pay for itself. So much for the naysayers.

The bank grew to other aspects of banking. Because it was a National Trust and Savings Association (NT&SA), with expansion limited to California, foreign markets became a target, as well as innovation in bank products and services. In those times, folks needing a car would have to have cash or borrow on credit from the Car Financing Dealers. Interest rates of 15% to 25% were the standard at the time. BofA turned that around by creating time/term borrowing as an efficient and far more economic method. I still remember it, in my time – as nostalgia hits me right in my heart – the customers coming with their auto loan coupon books with twenty-four, thirty-six or forty-eight coupons, to meet their monthly payment. Ripping out the appropriate coupon, we would dutifully stamp the stub "paid." People were proud to meet their obligations. We bankers were happy to be of help and to gain honest profits.

Writing checks only became a useful dynamic tool for consumers after, in the mid fifties, BofA and Stanford Institute of Technology developed "magnetic ink encoding" capabilities. This technology is often taken for granted. Pick up a sample from your check book and do a little exercise. While the whole body of the check contains the basic elements of legal negotiability – when, where, who draws, to whom, a dollar amount in both versions (numerical and written) and your signature – at the very bottom – the magnetically printed information is the most vital of all the elements in the check writing game. Now focus your eyes on the very bottom – from left to right - and you will detect numbers that reveal the number of the Federal Reserve Bank, the number of the Financial Institution, the unit number of the financial institution, the client's checking account number, the check number, and on the very right, the dollar amount of the check. In the fifties, less than twenty percent of the population possessed checking accounts. With this technology's processing and clearing capability, that number grew to almost ninety percent, just in a couple of decades. Bank of America, in the fifties, would process and clear tens of thousands of checks per day; in the eighties it was processing two to three dozen million. That's a lot of paper meeting the daily needs of consumers, businesses and government alike. Yes, government. The Federal Reserve Bank system benefited immensely by having access to a better, more accurate and faster way of measuring the money supply. Without it, economies of scale could never be achieved; consumer convenience would be fundamentally altered. Currently, magnetic ink, such as bar codes, is used in every business, retail or otherwise, but the application is somewhat different than MICR reading technology. For frequent air travelers the printing of your own "check in" document is a welcome convenience. One gets the idea that MICR (Magnetic Ink Character Recognition) in some manner got the ball rolling.

Another enormously important convenience is the credit card. The Bankamericard became another symbol, a nice companion to the check, in the transformation of tools available to us to move money and effect payments. Before Bank of America's Bankamericard, many other types of cards, mostly made of hard paper, existed and were used by a few financial institutions and retailers. However, these were of limited value and scope; they only reached a few thousand users. The Bankamericard was a different animal - kind of a wild horse, now domesticated and tamed - but once it was unleashed, it had and has the potential to cause many headaches. It was an "all purpose" card, in plastic with the colors blue and white, like its successor, the VISA card. It also represented the pride of a dignified institution.

The card was launched in the very early 1960s. A few years later, suffering growing pains and still a loss leader, it became a separate entity, now under the name of BankAmerica Service Corporation. Its popularity attracted the competition, and after litigation it became available to all banks. With all banks aboard and enjoying tremendous success, VISA became an iconic and world-recognized name. Even if it is not that "other card" one can accept the notion not-to-leave-home-without-it. Despite the various and polarizing views we have of the credit card, it is a good tool, if handled with care. So I use it liberally, but with care.

Bad winds will delay ships from reaching their destination, or imperil their voyages. The banking industry had benefitted from good winds filling theirs sails for many years. They did not prepare for the bad winds to come, and they steered the ship badly once the wind was in their face. A lack of good leadership got BofA into bad straits in the very late 1970s and early 1980s. It coincided with the deregulation of financial institutions and the bail-out debacle of Savings and Loan Associations. Wall Street, then as now, was out of control. Dramatic and unplanned changes in the financial universe can catch financial leaders with their pants down. Certainly, to be seen in ugly underwear is a little embarrassing. Literally on its knees, BofA was able to regain its stride and its prominence of old. Good leadership did that. Everybody gained: consumers, employees and shareholders. What a difference good leadership makes.

I am always fascinated by great, or even just solid, leadership. In my seven decades of living I have seen it all. I have also learned that employees or workers do not ruin a company. Leaders do that. There are those companies that make history; others bring misery. Bank of America had earned the right to respect and fame. Currently, what we get is shame. It is so sad. It did not have to be this way.

*Clockwise – Tony, Donalda, Victor, John
and Carlos. John's 65th birthday.*

18

Christmas Dinner and Backpack Culture

When a man sits with a pretty girl for an hour, it feels like a minute.
But let him sit on a hot stove for a minute and it's longer than any hour.
That's relativity.

Albert Einstein

I cannot seriously claim that a Christmas dinner and the backpack culture go hand-in-hand. Yet I needed one story to trigger the other. I cannot predict that this title will elicit curiosity and motivate the reader to invest a few more minutes on this chapter, rather than move on to the next. Ah, you will not skip it; you will go on reading because it is delicious; it is about family, like a family Christmas dinner.

In our family of three boys it was not unusual – and this is now spreading to the new generation - to be comfortable with the "hand-me-downs" culture. At least in those times, the seventies, eighties and nineties, when our sons were growing up, the high priced gadgets were age differentiated. If you bought a toy for one you did not have to buy the same for the other. The other would wait. There were toys and gadgets with different age appeal and utilization. In our home, there was an unequivocal culture and conviction that we did not live poorly, but we did not have money to waste. Money always had its uses and applications. The source of money was always clearly explained. Later on, as the boys grew from one age bracket to the next, they were expected to contribute to the same source. Eventually, they would come to gloat that they had been, reluctantly or not, a component of that source. Our sons always had what kids they associated with had, but not the best, or more important, not the most expensive. If I could rewind time, and had to raise them in our current environment, I would be broke; or maybe I would just have to give my kids away. The gap in ages from the first to the last son is three and one half years from the first to the second; six and one half years from the second to the last. Logically, stuff that was good and durable, not the flashy, poorly-made stuff, would be bequeathed to the next one.

Later on in years, since I am shorter than they are, some "hand-me-downs" would find their way to me as "hand-me-ups." Why not? After all, their tastes were better and more contemporary than mine. Oh, stories abound when my sons would make fun of me or fun of the clothes that I wore. Let's not go there. Those were great times; happy memories.

Last Christmas dinner was held at the home of my oldest son, Carlos. As the patriarch of our family, in another cultural setting these feasts would be staged at my home. We have hosted some, but at Donalda's and my age it is more convenient to have them at their homes. Besides, all of our sons have in-laws who mesh well with everyone else, so their homes become more authentic and appealing. So it was that all of our sons, spouses and grandkids and some in-laws gathered for a good Christmas meal. At one point of the gathering, perhaps dessert time or that time afterward when everyone gets up and moves around, I asked my youngest, Tony, if I could use his backpack again on my next journey. This journey will include three ladies: my wife, my oldest daughter-in-law, another female friend, and my friend Viegas. (Of course, Viegas.)

I had borrowed his backpack for my *Camino* of 2011. Actually Tony insisted that his backpack was far more functional than mine, and since I would be walking more days this time, it would be a better fit. My backpack - older, previously used - even with its multi-pockets, it was no match for Tony's. Bigger in size and volume, Tony's backpack was damn good. I guess it still is darn good, for I have taken good care of it, i.e., stored it right.

Contrary to what an experienced pilgrim advised at the American Friends of the *Camino* Gathering, I rarely saw a small backpack on a pilgrim's back. I even saw one pilgrim carrying his – and perhaps his wife's - belongings in a carry-on case. At the least, I saw and exchanged smiles with this man for over five stages. I also saw backpack-less folks – six of them – all yoga adherents, who routinely practiced yoga before the stage began or at some point at the end of afternoon, doing their 20-30 minute ritual. But although that experienced and credentialed pilgrim with three *Caminos* (800kms each) in three different seasons of the year like spring, summer and winter (yes, winter in northern Spain, hello; anybody there?) swore his life on it, a small backpack was rarely seen. Seriously, he claimed with a straight face that his tiny backpack was the only one any pilgrim needed. This guy was not and is not nuts, he comes across as being knowledgeable about the *Caminos* and life in general. At the gathering, during his half hour presentation, with his (still in good appearance) backpack on the ground surrounded by what all else would be housed in it, he tantalized all of us students - I guess I was a student for I pretended to want to learn something – with the meticulous steps of fitting everything in. No, he is not nuts. However on the matter of shoes or what you put on instead of bare feet, his recommendations would be challenged by another credible walker, also making a similar presentation. While the former believed in light walking shoes or sandals, similar to the ones he wore during the three day gathering, the latter did recommend boots. Good, well fitted boots; but boots, period. In any case my own backpack is good, for it is bigger than the former presenter's but smaller than Tony's.

"Of course, Pops, you can have it; or keep it; I have very little use for it now," replied Tony. Nearby, the middle son, Victor, was listening to the exchange and turned to his brother. "Did you buy a new backpack? What happened to the one I let you borrow in 2002? I guess you lost it, as I recall."

"No, I did not buy anything new," Tony blurted meekly. Pause turned into silence, more inquisitive silence, (yes, silence can be inquisitive) and the body language of the moment indicated that we would have a long conversation. As Victor's curiosity became patently clear, Tony dragged out his answer. "I thought that Dad knew the backpack was yours; I guess I told him then."

"How could you con me into believing you had lost it?" Victor's tone projected sheer brotherly authority. Did Tony con him? The occasion was not the ideal time to find out.

Victor was not finished. "It cost me one hundred twenty pounds (British pounds), and I'm thinking that my hard earned money has gone to waste." In jest or in truth, Victor's dollars are always part of any equation. One hundred twenty pounds would stay in my brain for a long while; Victor would not let that piece of history vanish any time soon. No wonder he is the one with wealth. Different blood, for sure.

The conversation went well. The grins and chuckles were like Christmas gifts, there were no punches thrown, and I became the "hand-me-up" guy. Lucky me - I know it will cost me something at some point in time, but it will be a price I can bear.

In reality we have three good sons, endowed with a variety of our traits and the traits of their grandparents spread nicely between them. These and some more acquired qualities on their own have proved to serve them well, making them good citizens of the global village.

୬∼ ∼ଡ଼

"Do not start a long walk without a backpack" is not a slogan, but it is now an ingrained habit that ranks almost as high as having good walking shoes. For me, this fascination has evolved into wanting to know about the history of backpacking. Who the heck cares about the history of backpacking? As long as there are stores that sell them, (every store does) is what counts; now, at this moment and this time. Whether you choose Wal-Mart, which is way cheaper, or REI or Sports Authority or even the boutique-type stores, it makes no difference.

I have my own version of the history of backpacking. Perhaps it is shaped by recollections of my own time backpacking, or my imaginings of what it could have been. I wanted to supplement these with some research via Google, Wikipedia and similar sites. Of the many I searched, one source, by Anja Knorr, provided the simplest of the interpretations. Whether Anja authorizes me or not, I will share a couple of Anja's paragraphs; just for flavor.

> "Backpacking has been around for quite some time now. Some guys themselves have been doing it for decades. I got talking to people who have done some backpacking and none actually seem to know how it all began. Everyone can recall, and with lots of happy memories, how it started for them but it was more of a mystery when it came to the very history of backpacking."

Here is another nice interpretation:

> "Man has been a traveler for a long time. As a matter of fact we were nomadic when we started. But that won't fit the bill here. That was a way of life, more of a compulsion than a choice. Maybe those guys preferred to stay put as a recreational
>
> activity. So, that as history is out of the question."

I like her words "nomadic" and "guys". I take these to mean we - just men - were always on the run, carrying our possessions and those of the ladies. Of course, what are men for?

> "Another popular view considers the role played by the Hippies in the 1960s and the 70s. They definitely were the people who moved around a lot that too along fixed locales and do leave enough hints for having influenced the backpacking tradition."

This last quote is even more relevant to me. It defines the era, strangely enough, when I became a productive citizen. I love it, for it has more personal meaning; that culture gave birth to, or turned to be the precursor of, many cultures in our present times.

ᔑ᠊ᢀ

The importance of memories is amazing. They come to hit us or elevate and elate us with incredible warm feelings. I feel nourished by these feelings. Memories do not bring food to the table, but like Jesus said "Man does not live by bread alone." I am warm with memories now.

I do not recall a backpack of any kind in any normal way of life during my childhood. In my first recollections, around my first decade of existence, I remember that two or three rich kids carried their school books in a satchel. My first vivid memories of backpacks are fixed on the military – the infantry men; and now infantry women, too.

The Azores islands –remember those nine dots in the middle of the Atlantic – where about a quarter million people make their home (and they are my home, during two or three summer months) – were at one point, during WWII, very strategically important to America as well as to the European Allies. In fact, the Azores were also of great importance during the Israeli/Arab war in the sixties. With the US fully engaged in the war in Europe, the need to supply our troops with everything a war requires was primarily fulfilled by ships via the ocean that separates the two continents. Smack right in the middle of the Atlantic – squarely between the US east coast and Europe's southern west coast, lie the Azores. Two thousand miles (give or take a hundred) to the west is America and a thousand plus to the east. No planes at that time, cargo planes that is, were available to transport the millions and millions of tons of military and related supplies needed to support our troops. The Azores, a region belonging to Portugal, fit that bill. Portugal, officially neutral in the war, but married to the British in some manner, relinquished its position, or had no choice but to cave in and allow both the US and GB to use that war theatre in any capacity. Of course, Portugal played both roles nicely, helping the Allies with this strategic geographic arena, and supplying the Nazis with food products. I do not know what one calls these roles, but in my book it has a bad smell. Salazar, the mild dictator governing Portugal then, was astute, but perhaps also sleazy.

The Atlantic Ocean was free for all navigation and the convoys of American supply ships traversing the Azorean waters were sweet targets of the German submarines. And that's when the islands, innocent bystanders, became victims, as the errant torpedoes missed the ships and hit land. If they hit their targets, it would cripple the ships, pushing them towards land. I still remember seeing the signs of those "cat-and-mouse" games. The house windows were taped up in areas around the coast – naturally most of the population lived around the coast –with the tape reinforcing the glass diagonally, or crisscrossed like a wooden lattice. I must have also heard the torpedoes, when they missing the target, hit the coast and produce thunder so that even the taped windows felt threatened. On the other hand, babies or toddlers do not recall these things. I was a baby then.

San Miguel, the largest by far of all the islands, became home to more than the usual military contingents. Primarily Portuguese military, these troops were a constant reminder that war could hit our shores in some fashion. I do recall that for years more than a dozen of the ship's smokestacks remained visible landmarks near the coastline, scenic icons as the result of war maneuvers. Relics of the war, these smokestacks stood above the water line for years. In the years following the war, the military did not vanish quickly. Another, more constrained war was emerging as the real, physical one was becoming history. The military presence on the islands would take its time to extinguish itself, and so one could see troops – companies or battalions - moving from their base to other areas of the island, where four to five days of exercises would occupy their time. And it was around this time – the late forties – that I saw the troops, in mass formation, with all their fire power and support equipment, like moving kitchens in the military vehicles and horse drawn carts, marching towards their training camps. The military men, including the infantry, were ready for their four or five day vacation.

A military uniform almost always brings out the best of emotions in citizens. I got emotional when I heard the sound of the trumpets or the drums far away, coming down the main street where everything was transacted. Rushing from my own street to the main street, I would see the soldiers wearing their regalia and bearing, nicely bound over their backs, the topic of this conversation – the backpack. Real backpacks, with compartments for everything a soldier would need for their four-five day odyssey. Those backpacks must have meant a lot to them. I'll bet they did.

సౌ ✋

My second backpack recollection dates back to 1991 – our 25th wedding anniversary year – when my wife insisted on celebrating with a visit to the Pope. Yes, our real and dear Catholic Pope, John Paul II. There was no private audience for two, or even a dozen; we were in his presence as part of an audience of about five thousand in the Vatican auditorium.

Of course we did not travel lightly; quite the opposite. Thus a backpack was remotely removed from our luggage list. Going to the Vatican - according to my wife - required two additional suitcases. Why? I still have no clue or explanation and I do not even dare ask. Unless Donalda thought that the Pope would invite her to subsequent audiences on the same trip.

Fortunately, a miracle occurred. I found a solution to the luggage excesses, which enabled us to continue on with our other days of vacation, still somewhat sane. Donalda will have a rude awakening as she does her own *Camino* with just the help of a backpack. Good luck to her, and me, when we deal with her frustration at travelling light. We will see.

This 25th wedding anniversary trip took twenty one days, with Italy as the main geographic pleasure, eight days of Eurail time and travel, five days of car rental, and the rest on our blessed feet. It was during the longest segment of our rail trip that we became acquainted with the backpacking culture. It is enormously difficult to transmit the images of the oceans of backpackers, their many aspects and scenes, onto paper and with the color they deserve. For us, at that time, it was an "awe thing".

Everyone knows that unlike America, Europe depends heavily on mass transit. If Europeans equally love their four-wheelers, mass transit delivers what we will never deliver on a large scale or in consistent and effective ways. Blame no one or many, but this is what it is. I will be dead, so will be the generation of my kids, if and when America (even taking into account New York and Chicago) has a decent mass transit system. Perhaps by then – decades and decades away - mass transit will be comprised of earthlings and the like navigating in the open, but inevitably very congested, skies.

Our first leg of the train trip started in Rome and ended in Paris. Much later, towards the end part of our stay in Italy, we saw that Rome was also inundated with backpackers. The minute we stopped at one of the three largest intercontinental train stations, in Paris, we were confronted with these waves of backpackers. My Lord, is it that the whole world is traveling Europe this way? What ever happened to the carry-on, and Donalda's big pieces of luggage? Can you really carry your three-piece suit, fine ties, shined shoes, long dresses and an assortment of make-up stuff in a backpack? Are you are kidding me?!

No, no one was kidding anybody. The backpacker, as I know now, does not carry normal belongings with him or her. They carry just the essentials; ask the hippies of the 60s or a *Camino* pilgrim. From three days in Paris, the Eurail voyage extended to Portugal, where we stayed with our friends for another three days. It was on the return train trip from Lisbon to Rome that we were struck by the idea; what a beautiful, artistic and clever way to travel as a duo; like a couple of lovers, or husband and wife.

Our tickets were for second class travel, the tickets that backpackers can afford. Some even manage to travel at some lower level or free. The carriage or compartment can fit six. For the most part until we changed trains in Spain, the carriage was occupied by Donalda and me and another couple, who we learned later were Swedish. Donalda and I sat side by side until we recognized that there were only four in the carriage, then we switched to sit on opposite sides. Slowly leaving Santa Apolonia, a large train station in Lisbon, the train soon gained normal speed, and half dozen hours later would take us through Spain and into French territory.

Experienced in these types of travel, the Swedish couple knew what to do. We did not. Both carried hefty backpacks but the male, the immortal male, carried more stuff. His had more compartments and pockets and God knows what else. We had had a decent meal with our friends and were prepared to endure twelve hours of just snacking. The Swedish couple had other plans - the methods backpackers know.

They sat neatly and squarely opposite each other, their knees practically touching each other for positioning and leverage, (nothing else – no footsie stuff) –when the male pulls (I recall well) from one of the compartments, a small cutting board. I cannot recall what material: wood or plastic; it does not matter. As far I know, it could have been a cutting board purchased at an IKEA store, a store that their own countrymen had invented and exported to the large global village. With both knees covered with the cutting board, they looked ready to initiate the "Bon appetite." Once aligned, he pulls out a large loaf of Portuguese artisan bread (a two pounder?). Next come the cheese, and then a large roll of "looks like and is not like salami", perhaps "chourição" (a Portuguese version of Italian dry copa).

His utility knife is something I can relate to. Swiss or not, these are great utility tools many a walker or hiker will use. The bread cut into adequate portions, the cheese and salami sliced to perfection, spread neatly over the board, a fortified meal - dinner by now - was about to take center stage. We would be witnesses to this colorful show. The beer was the next component of the meal: a 1plus liter bottle of Portuguese beer, fetched from another compartment of the backpack, was pulled out, unscrewed and passed along from one to another and so on, until it was fully consumed.

Moments later, after exchanging glances, we made some conversation. With their limited English, the conversation was not enlarged, but their glances and smiles were obvious and sincere. At least we knew they were Swedish, a little past their thirties, but we can't fathom if they were married or living together. After all the Swedish, like their brethren Scandinavians, in addition to cars, domestic appliances, IKEA, and the cell phone, would invent the experimentation of living together for two dozen years before tying the knot. We had a few .375 liter bottles of Portuguese wine with us. We offered a couple of them, which they gratefully accepted and gulped. What a backpack that man had! Amen, I say.

Eventually I would compare their trip to similar trips that Victor, in 1995, and Tony, in 2002, would take throughout Europe once their eight-month stays in London were over. I did not have to ask them how the trips went. Both had earned their money for such economy-budgeted trips, and used these opportunities to see the world a little and up close. Donalda and I had witnessed good examples of such journeys. Great for them.

John & Donalda's seven grandchildren

John & Donalda's grandchildren, sons and daughters-in-law

19

The Power of the Word, the Power of Our Own Miracles

Be the change you wish to see in the world.

Ghandi

When I was reaching the end of my last paragraph, mostly about backpacking culture, I got caught up in the moment and I was still motivated to share a few more ideas and interpretations of the origins of backpacking. It was getting late and the knowledge that I would miss another chance to do my four-mile walk was not sitting well with me. I know, this is winter and even in California it is cold outside. The outdoors, other than for romantic reasons, is not appealing. My warm socks and loafers, ever-present old sweat pants and shirt, and a warm mug of hot tea, complete the fine arrangement of a late morning and afternoon.

However, I did stop what I was doing and went for my four mile walk. I felt good and a little liberated. Instead of dressing my head with the also-ancient hand radio, connected to the old-fashioned headphones, my head was covered this time only with an old 49ers hat. The headphones resemble the ones that football head coaches wear on the sidelines. Well, minus the microphone. I have no one to give orders or instructions via remote control; or more important, direct plays. Don't let this 49ers affiliation stop you from reading my notes. I am a fair-weather fan. I wish no harm, and these present times are unique, the Niners are golden and I am filled with the appropriate Bay Area football fever. It is about time that the dynasty returns. On my solo walks - Donalda and I walk at times together - I usually carry my WWII era radio and invariably tune to KNBR sports or KGO talk shows and news stations. I am waiting for my I-musical thing for Christmas. Of course with the good news about the Niners, it is easy for a (fair-weather) fan to choose KNBR over KGO. News will come later. Far from being a sports radio talk show junkie I still, when music or news do not turn me on, tune to KNBR occasionally.

The Niners phenomenon brought excitement, not only because they are playing well, turning their previous miserable seasons of futility into positions of contention, but more for the type of their success. This, instigated by a proven leader with "blue collar" techniques like those of a waterfront longshoreman, is the result of a very effective use of the power of the word. Devoid of vanity or pomposity, followers have become believers, creating an extraordinarily powerful "whole." While just four or five weeks ago the Niners were slowly turning naysayers into believers, now conversations about playing in the Super Bowl are very much the thing. According to the players, when asked about the dramatic turn-around, their unvarnished answers are like those of a blue color worker, not reflecting the "awe" thing. The inspirational speeches or motivations typically credited for such turnarounds are absent in their answers. The interviewers allude to these transformations; the players do not buy such talk or theories. Quite on the contrary; the players claim that the previous coach was an outstanding speaker and motivator, better than Harbaugh. Their infatuation with Harbaugh and the current leadership regimen seems to rest on the belief that words properly used, at the right time, with honesty and candor, can move mountains. Whether the 49ers win a play-off game, reach, or even win the Super Bowl, is not entirely important. What is and has been important is that the players embraced and executed the "team" concept and held the extraordinary belief that the team is far greater than any single piece of the puzzle. The whole is greater, is above the individual. This has been a great season; not only on the football field with its good outcomes, but also because it has revealed the power of a good word.

I was without a radio, with a free and open mind, and the environment invited more thinking. Not a good prescription for a tired mind, but what else to do? The late afternoon was on the verge of turning darkness quickly, with crisp, overcast weather that was refreshingly appealing. It was nice to get out and feel the cold tickle my legs and blush my cheeks. Although I always like to change walking itineraries – to observe and experience different surroundings – the night was approaching, so the pleasure of scenic variety was not there. A longer walk helps to vary the scenery. San Ramon at night is no downtown San Francisco; there are no flashy signs, no old or charming neighborhoods. (Tourists do not come to San Ramon, either.) Yet, walking the various routes during the rush time does inspire new observations and different thinking. People rushing, drivers who do not keep their eyes on the pedestrians, the timing of light signals, the parking lots of the shopping centers, again with rushed shoppers, all become the casts of soap operas. There may be no plots worth remembering, but these are shows of their own kind.

❧ ❧

I chose the title for this chapter, the penultimate, to be "The Power of the Word, the Power of Our Own Miracles" because I am a believer in the power of the word and that all of us are miracle makers. Seriously, I believe in both theories. I cannot recall where I read the following quote, something about the human soul and spirit, but it sounded like this: "In all my years of living I have observed some vanity and selfishness in people; yet, I also have come to believe that part of the human soul and spirit, if and when unleashed, has the capacity for great acts of love and caring." Certainly I have had bouts with my own faith, and perhaps my beliefs, more often than not; yet I found strength to give it another try once I got back on my feet.

There are thousands of books on motivation and others more on inspirational speeches, speeches that became reference material for the ages; all of them relying on the power of the word. Some words stuck while others faded away; they lost their meaning and value. Like money misspent, words that misfired because they were insincere or not meant to be right, lost their value. I, too, was deeply affected by the good, honest use of the word during my career and personal life. These words were as refreshing as the cold water from a clean brook on a hot day.

All the important vignettes in this extraordinary year were built on gestures, touches and mostly on words uttered at the right moment with an honest emphasis. Without them the glue that keeps our lives intact would slowly lose its power, its effect.

In spite of a very busy year I still had time to revisit my own little, meager library consisting of only a few shelves with books. Donalda's dozens of novels from Nora Roberts, Nicholas Sparks, Jodi Picoult together with a few religious books (what a mix) are scattered all over. Blame it on lack of space. (Just kidding.) Thinking that this year could be the breaking point, as in, do it or don't do it, I started browsing some books to shake up my thoughts, inspire my senses, trigger my writing appetite. It was a good journey and one of the books contained great material relating to many matters, including the power of the word. Amongst books and tapes from Tom Peters, the business guru, Dr. Wayne Dyer, motivational speaker, from Warren Buffet and Mother Teresa, one book by Father Anthony De Melo (no relation to me), a Jesuit, caught my attention. Father De Melo's presentations – full of common sense and some humor - always make us feel, or at least I wonder, why I didn't think of that *that* way? It is so simple and practical. As I was leafing through a few pages, a couple of paragraphs piqued my interest. I share them here:

> A Finish farmer, at the time when they were drawing the borders between Finland and Russia, was at a crossroads, trying to decide whether to be Russian or Finish. After some thought, he decided to be Finish, but he did not want to offend the Russians. When he was confronted by the Russians about why he chose Finland, he replied, "It has been always my desire to live in Mother Russia, but at my age, I would not survive another Russian winter."

Father de Melo explains that "Russia" and "Finland" are just words. Nothing changed with the farmer, but the selection of words to justify his decision.

Again, from Father Anthony de Melo:

> A guru was once trying to explain to a crowd how human beings react to words, how they live on words, rather than on reality. One of the men stood up and protested. He said, "I do not agree that words have much effect on us." The guru said, "Sit down, you son of a bitch." The man went livid with rage and said, "You call yourself an enlightened person, a guru, a master, but you ought to be ashamed of yourself." The guru then said, "Pardon me, sir, I was carried away. I really beg your pardon; that was a lapse; I'm sorry." The man finally calmed down. Then the guru said: "It took just a few seconds to stir the whole tempest within you; and it took just a few words to calm you down, didn't it?"

જ્જ

Miracles have a definition of their own. In the Catholic Church miracles are part of our catechism, our history and that reservoir of beliefs. No saint is canonized without having, not one, but many miracles attributed to him or her. I have no canon law knowledge or even the foggiest idea of how miracles are identified, documented, catalogued, or awarded. Whatever I know is derived from word of mouth, some reading and so on. Before I add a few of my thoughts I must disclaim that I have not done any research on the matter; perhaps I should have. Or perhaps not, as this is equally a safe route. Whatever I write can be labeled as an opinion from an ordinary and somewhat ignorant human being; at least on this matter.

So if canonization requires miracles and if the Catholic Church is replete with saints one can infer that miracles occur regularly. All of us, even others like average agnostics, claim on a regular basis that this or that was the result of a miracle. It was a miracle that he caught that ball, escaped that disaster, did not miss the train, or a very long list of occasions and occurrences that happen in anyone's life. If some are trivially stated, many others are seriously examined by ourselves or others, with enough conviction to make a saint take notice.

I have taken notice of many (small) miracles in my life and I have also observed unbelievable outcomes in others' lives, on the borderline of miracles from above. I have heard some truly inspirational stories. All of this causes me to believe that we – ourselves – have the power of miracle making. I guess God, in His infinite knowledge and power, endowed human beings with everything physical about us, and then something else that can be interpreted as being supernatural. I have seen pictures of hearts pumping but not of hearts loving; these are felt. I have seen energy wrapping us in many ways, although not a picture of a soul or spirit. I have felt that instead. Well, the philosophers and theologians can define that. Like I said, I have done no research. Help me, St. Augustine.

I am not talking about the miracle of a passenger that was set to fly in one of the planes that crashed on September 11, in one of those flights of infamy; nor the one or two employees that did not go to work on that day, who for no apparent reason did not set foot in one of the World Trade towers. I do not claim these to be miracles, for the same reason that many others perished.

A few years back, during my consulting days, I was driving with one of the business owners. He went on a litany of complaints, a lament that everything was going wrong with him and his business. Nothing he touched, he claimed with much conviction, was hitting the mark. Everything that could go wrong did; perhaps somebody had laid a curse on him. I guess his favorite cause for his problems was a curse; that was the culprit he was trying to drive into my skull. As the conversation progressed (it was now getting a life of its own, with some colors) he compared his bad luck to times of the past when people were confronted with similar misery. In those times, he recalled, people would fight curses by availing themselves of the services offered by spiritual readers, fortune tellers or voodoo priests or just modern shrinks.

I was aware of his business structure, and I recognized that he had the power to tweak a few things here or there. His notion of a curse was too much for me. I guess I needed to earn my pay, because I found the only credible solution. I told him that the solution was within him. My advice was simple, and it fell to him: his courage was real, his knowledge well proven, and the people around him had the capacity to rally around him and cause different and prosperous results. The miracle was within him – he was the miracle maker. In retrospect, I should have billed him for my solution; for he did not spend a dime with the fortune teller.

It does not take a rocket scientist to know that we have the power of the miracle. We just need awareness and the will to make it happen. We can make these miracles happen, first with us, and then with everyone around us. After all, God did not shower us with these gifts just to be wasted.

20

Wrapping Up the Year

I am more and more convinced that man is a dangerous creature;
And that power, whether vested in many or a few,
Is ever grasping, and like the grave, cries "Give, Give!"

Abigail Adams (letter to John Adams, 1775)

The year is coming to a close and I realize that my project is reaching its destination. I am glad and also relieved. What started as a tentative undertaking, with a struggle at mid-point when my doubts about writing surfaced, has now become the finished product – a collage of many images and touches in one year - 2011. I wish to think it also looks like a nice quilt.

As I reviewed my notes and matched them to the paragraphs and chapters, and as I butchered many of the parts with revisions, I concluded that in the end, this project resembled, metaphorically speaking, a bowl of minestrone soup. The difference between one or another rests on the flavors. If you have the minimum of cooking skills, and some patience to read the recipe cooking steps, you will not be able to mess up or ruin minestrone soup. The amalgamation of all the ingredients - and there are many in minestrone soup - with its diverse properties and colors, with the proper cooking steps, always turns into a good and delicious meal. Perhaps I am fantasizing that my project has attained the same results. Give me some slack - I am in the learning stages; this is my first writing project.

2011, the first year of the second decade, has been extraordinary for me, yet I was hoping it would be more hopeful and better than the previous decade. The previous decade was clearly a decade of waste. What a way to begin the new century, the new decade, with such an unnecessarily ugly legacy.

Not satisfied with the dot.com implosion, and the shenanigans of Enron and company, we had to embark on a war that did not merit our taxpayer's dollars and/or the alienation of our allies in Europe and elsewhere in the world. What a waste of human intelligence and lives. The highly symbolic but emblematic truth of reality in Theodore Roosevelt's quote "Speak softly and carry a big stick; you will go far" fell into the deaf ears of many of our political leaders. That slogan is still ignored or unread by many who should take heed.

Everyone on our planet knows extremely well that America has mighty military power and has proved to know how to use it. We do not need to constantly advertise it, or more importantly, to rub our allies' or enemies' noses in it to establish their fear. We don't, plain and simple. In fact, brandishing our pistols like Texas cowboys or John Wayne challenging Wyatt Earp to a duel is not the prescription for rational solutions. Do we really want to see a scenario such as the fight at the O K Corral? What happened to our brain power?

At least one good thing has happened this year. The current administration, in the face of these challenges, has been a living proof that "whispering softly and having the big stick" will take us far. Proof exists that we can also resolve many conflicts very effectively with little of the taxpayer's money, and no loss of our human assets, our people. More so, the world looks at us more confidently, and they are more enamored of our brain power. Intelligent, quiet and effective diplomacy, matched by timely fire power, has done the job.

Just step back a few years to the last decade. We had Afghanistan, a war theater just for ourselves – we were the de facto owners – and Osama Bin Laden within our grasp, yet he was never caught. This had nothing to do with the military or what happens in the business world with employees or workers. It was leadership that failed. Finally, with less fanfare - just recently, last May - with the guns still in our holsters, the grand prize of the terrorism world became ours. The same military – quietly and softly – got the job done. Go figure it. I am resigned to think that many others are in denial.

A few days to 2012, and the news is the same: not good, less bad but still causing pessimism graduating to indifference and indifference into resignation. Only the fringe groups maintain their drum beat, spewing noises that make you want to throw up. All along these sounds are accompanied by shows of finger pointing and the blame game. Impotence could take the upper hand. I hope not, for even if I do not see any Abraham Lincolns or Franklin Roosevelts or AP Gianninis around the corner, men of good will eventually will show up. That's my faith in the human spirit and the miracle makers. The others will find their own fate.

The year is definitely coming to a close. For some reason, people make resolutions for the New Year: give up smoking, shed more pounds, be nicer to their mate, not to hit the dog or simply, to keep their mouth shut. As for me, normally I make no resolutions. If I find myself incapable of addressing serious issues affecting my life during the year at a relevant time, the New Year should not have that power of change.

Well, now I have broken the mold – I will make a resolution. It aims at combating what has been gnawing at me for a long time. Like many of us, I carry excess baggage – whether physical, emotional, spiritual or whatever. Being creatures of habit, our real, figurative, invisible baggage has a subtle way of penetrating our existence, nestling comfortably to stay within us, regenerating as if it is part of ourselves, our personalities.

My baggage or junk centers on two fronts: the real and visible, and the spiritual. My garage is my visible one. Anyone walking into my garage can tell it is. The other is my inner life, my world of the ordinary, of the mysterious, and the world of spiritual confusion.

I recall many years ago when my father used to visit me every two to three years and stay with us for three to four weeks. He lived in Canada, Brampton. He was proud of Donalda and me and the way we took charge of our lives and raised our kids. But with this praise also came his consternation that we lived a very hectic life – always busy moving from one station of our programmed life to another. Although he would not predict whether we would live a short or prolonged life, he ventured to say that our hearts were taking a beating. Well I am over seventy by now and I think I am okay. He lived to be eighty-eight. His observations and advice still ring well in my ears and my mind as a guide to be more careful with the amount of weight and perhaps luggage I choose to carry.

On a funny note, on one of those visits, he pulled me aside in my garage. He rested his arm on my shoulder and towed me around from zero to three hundred sixty degrees, stopping at one point or another, and with his finger pointed at several spots. The things I had stored there were mostly no good. In other words, moving our attention and eyes full circle, one could classify that everything was basically junk material. "This should go out, that too, or that even burned." He added, "Ask for a dump box and just throw away one thing after another." In my early years this would have hurt my feelings. But not when he made those observations. In fact many times, exasperated that I could not locate one tool here, a certain size nail or screw there, I would run to the hardware store to purchase what I needed. Sure enough, hours or days later I would find what I was missing. Yeah, we know the story. He was right and perhaps he had also been wrong at one stage of his life. These learning processes repeat themselves.

I guess that once I finish cleaning my garage of everything I accumulated through the years of thinking I would need them one day, then I will turn my attention to my computer. The files are bursting at the seams. They must go, too.

I can use all of these reasons and pretexts and benefit from these resolutions. But like in the years past, I will rather pray to the Lord for more enlightenment, more awareness and fortitude to live my age, my aging process. Liberation must be joyful, too.

~ ~ ~ To put the world in order we must first put the nation in order;

To put the nation in order, we must first put the family in order;

To put the family in order, we must first cultivate our personal life;

We must first set our hearts right. ~ ~ ~

Confucius

Notes, References, Credits And Disclaimers

I do have a few friends to thank for their help during the process of reviewing this project – reading, correcting spelling and offering appropriate suggestions. In a special way my thanks are directed at my good friend Carlos Almeida. Not only because he participated in the proof reading and related review but more for encouraging me to go to the end. Also my gratitude to Diane Pierotti, my good friend and former associate when we worked at Bank of America, for a masterfully designed book cover. So thanks to all for your help; without it the end result would not be as satisfying. Or it might have received a less favorable reaction from my writing and publishing tutor, Nancy Barnes. I was happy to learn about her and to have received the kind of professional support a neophyte needs. I hope that I have a chance at another writing project and that Nancy will be available to equally guide me on the finished product. Nancy is that talented and nice to work with.

I had my wife in mind to thank, for she participated in all the experiences that excited me in 2011. Besides, believe it or not, her silence itself gave very positive approval as I spent many hours on the laptop; her smiles communicated bewilderment but also support. I valued this.

I thank all my friends both in America and Portugal, those with their own stories and tales; they represented the raw material for the book and the reason that a writing project came to be. I also thought of my grandkids, for in part, this book is dedicated to them.

I need to list some other important notes, to identify some references for the chapters where my statements imply the presence of facts, and also to disclaim any perceptions of misleading anyone.

In some chapters, and in particular the final one, contrary to my claim of having no grudges against the money changers or political power brokers, one can read that I am still bitter about the mess prevailing on our fragile planet. On one hand, I want to come across as being civilized and balanced in my views, on the other hand, as I talk with many people, I know that they all feel equally despondent with the status of things. Considering the political fervor and rhetoric from the extreme conservative group, and lamenting the quality (or lack of quality) of the candidates, I cannot help but cry out: "My Lord, do these people think they are qualified and capable of governing a nation of three hundred twenty million people, diversified to the hilt, in an environment of polarization, and where greed, incompetence and fraud are still the real drivers?" I don't care who governs next. Honestly, I don't. I truly pray that God intervenes in a clear (yet invisible as always) way and causes a miracle of change, where the honest, the caring, the humble, and the capable bring us and the rest of the global village to the promised land. Nothing else; I am tired of charlatans, impostors and hypocritical folks.

References

The chapter where I relate my career experiences at Bank of America contains much information you can regard as fact. Indeed, around the San Francisco earth quake of 1906, the dates and events were drawn from the book *Biography of a Bank – the History of Bank of America* by Marquis James and Bessie R. James, 1954.

Other data, about later years, was obtained via my contacts with old timers, some very proud Bank of America employees. For instance, I give credit for the MICR technology to Stanford Research Institute and Bank of America. I do not possess proof of how much B of A was involved in this technology. What I do know was related by the manager back in 1974 when I was assigned to the Fruitvale Branch in Oakland. Clifford Viery, the manager, used to marvel at Bank of America and what it represented to him. He had over forty years in his banking career and was ready to retire; I was the gullible recipient of his recollections of yesteryears. One of the recollections he would tell with vivid pride was that his brother, William, (I think), was one of the few members of the team that worked side by side with SRI on the project.

On matters of the *Camino*, all of the information provided reflects my own experiences. However, I feel indebted to John Brierly, author of the *Camino Guides*. There are many guides from equally credible sources. His covers far more information than any other guide I came to know. It goes beyond with enormous detail about stages, distances, meticulously drawn maps, and places to stay and eat. His experiences and devotion to everything about the *Camino*s are cleverly and warmly communicated. I would certainly recommend investing in the price of his guides and maps.

Disclaimer

Any disclaimer for this project would rest on the belief that everything we've learned and know was imparted by others. We are recipients of many lessons from those who preceded us, those who are with us and even others who have come after us. Some were great lessons, some not too great, and others bad enough to stay away from. After all, we are human beings.

Made in the USA
San Bernardino, CA
07 November 2017